Great Topics of the World

Great Topics of the World

Essays by
ALBERT GOLDBARTH

DAVID R. GODINE · PUBLISHER
Boston

First published in 1994 by
DAVID R. GODINE, PUBLISHER, INC.
BOX 9103
Lincoln, Massachusetts 01773

Library of Congress Cataloging-in-Publication Data
Great topics of the world : essays / by Albert Goldbarth. —1st ed.
p.   cm.
I. Title.
PS3557.0354G7 1994   814'.54—DC20   94-32002 CIP
ISBN 1-56792-017-9

First edition
Printed and bound in the United States of America

ACKNOWLEDGMENTS

"Delft" and "The Future" originally appeared in *The Kenyon Review;* "Delft" was also reprinted as a limited edition chapbook by Green-Tower Press. "The History of the Universe is Important to This Story" and "Worlds" originally appeared in *The New England Review.*

My thanks to the editors involved, especially Bill Trowbridge, Terry Hummer, Marilyn Hacker, David Baker, and David Huddle.

FOR SKYLER

Contents

…all the country and Europe was in arms, and the greatest event of history pending; and honest Peggy O'Dowd, whom it concerned as well as another, went on prattling about Ballinafad, and the horses in the stables at Glenmaloney, and the clar't drunk there; and Jos Sedley interposed about curry and rice at Dum-dum; and Amelia thought about her husband, and how best she should show her love for him; as if these were the great topics of the world.

—WILLIAM MAKEPEACE THACKERAY
Vanity Fair

Great Topics of the World

Delft

*No great and enduring volume can
ever be written on the flea, though
many there be who have tried it.*
HERMAN MELVILLE

*H*e cometh unto his kingdom now.
Yea, he cometh unto the greased posed-open body of his belovéd, Cornelia *nee* Swalmius, where she beckons from the alcove-bed, beneath the turkish rug flung coverlet-like for extra warmth, she of the variegated fleshy plains and amphitheatrical vastness, toe-nook, ear-maze, sweet crease under the arm, where tassel-bodied bacterial Creation loop-de-loops and only he of all gigantic unknowing humankind has witnessed its aswimming, dividing wonders. Call him Leeuwenhoek.

For the spit or the snot below his exemplary lenses is a living turkish rug, is a paisley of armies and harem houris, brigands, flagellating pilgrims, hosts and hordes, upon their skimpily cellular business. Say it LAY-wen-hook: with his pseudopods and gastropods and all the other podners in the enterprise of being alive at any glimmering instance on this planet, on up to pea pods

Mendel will duly contemplate later, and the *pas de deux* of the ovaries as they practice with each other for that moment they're asked to glide out star-showered onto the ballroom floor. An-TONY-van-LAY-wen-hook. "Here…"

For he, himself, is overmuch drunkenly groggy with having supped on her pungent dermal delights, although he knows her busy microcitizenry is going about its daily rounds clear-headedly, in alpine height, in swampy venetian recesses. O, the krill of her! The rotifers! The roe! "Yes, that's it…there."

For he has seen the populations of the cheesiness between her fine Dutch teeth—and in the pleasures of her lips, and in the wonders of the thronging animalcules therein, he revels with equally unblinking gusto, and of the pleasure he brings her in turn, he knows: that there are levels, and under them levels, and so on, crowded.

Yea, I lift my pen as baton to all of the congregate proboscises of the globe, that join in this one blatted honorific bombastic cockadoodle, for he is Leeuwenhoek, he has studied the spires and bristles, the mitred tips and galley-oared bellies, that pass beneath our notice.

Finished, lounging in the late Delft light in afterplay, "…an-other…another…" casually tweezing the seventeenth century's fleas from the folds of her body, cracking those tiny rhinocer-lings' sleek cases with his fingers.

～

It's altered everything thereafter. As did the atomic bomb, movable type, an accurate mirror: think of a life in which you'd never clearly seen your own face.

Leeuwenhoek made the world larger by making it smaller. He wasn't the first. We have no lens for looking back in time, but Zacharias Jansen, "an obscure spectacle-maker of Middleburg," is right now choice contender for its inventor. John Faber, naturalist and physician, named it "after the model of telescope, a microscope"—reminding us we zoomed the moon's craters before our own cankered insides. And Robert Hooke, in *Micrographia*, published 57 illustrations enabled by his new optical aid—describing the honeycomb structure of cork, he uses "cell" for the first time in its modern biological sense.

But Leeuwenhoek is the reverse-Galileo from whom it's most tempting to date the birth of a wholly new understanding. Before him, sight stopped at the dot of a flea. It wasn't of course that sight could *not* go further so much as that "further" didn't exist. Our vision through knowable space was infinite.

After Leeuwenhoek, vision was finite, simply because known space came into being at which the eyes' gaze failed.

The cosmos, which had been hierarchical, now was incremental. The difference this makes. The resonances.

The flea, which had been the final blank wall of the world became the door to a new world. There, the flea was a looming leviathan. We might call those units *fleas*, by which the space between two worlds is measured—and by which we leap across.

Then Columbus extended the European planet-map by (so-many) fleas.

Alicemay Axleburr—waking in her bed in the emergency ward of a Dayton, Ohio hospital after having been officially dead, now having light, albeit the bloodless wired-in ceiling light of her room, dance manic to hosannas in her eyes again—went out of her body by (so-many) fleas, with a round-trip ticket of ectoplasm, and made the (so-many) fleas return journey.

Yea, for he peereth long and long at this Animal Crumb and seeth both the End and the Beginning—and the compact Transport therefrom and thereto.

6 July: Worm formed out of egg.

*17 July: Worm white all over and did spin around itself a covering
web.*

21 July: Changed into a chrysalis of transparent white.

*25 July: Assumed somewhat a red colour, this growing evermore
deeper.*

*30 July: Entirely red, and in the evening the Flea it contained was
hopping about in the glass.*

~

They've only pestered me once in my life, and that was at Cynthia's, courtesy of a pug-snouted marmalade tabby so evolved toward feline unapproachability, sharing its fleas with us seemed its singlemost warmhearted gesture.

In those days, though, when love was new, and I was so new that my heart squeaked like a boot fresh from the box, and sex was new and each lick of a stamp or casual glance at the butcher's display-case of glistening organ-meats was fraught with recent memory of (and promise of yet more) wondrously offered-up sexual chowchow and marzipan…in those days, anything bringing me back to Cynthia's especially flawless surface with its neatly-trimmed (and indeed, near topiary-like) central gardenspot, was welcome. So I picked fleas off her, chasing them with a fox hunt ardor, suffering my own pink frieze of bites around the ankles as a necessary dues, and thanking that otherwise damnable cat for its smuggling-in of what seemed to be, in my godawful moon-eyed and drooly infatuee's vision, a bevy of cupid's helpers, each with its requisite arrow.

If this prose seems overlush—well, that's the boy I'm describing, now twenty years back. We'd roll, as full of the stuffings of lust as two *cannolis*, over the unkempt bed beneath the cheap print of Vermeer (his *View of Delft*) and some enraged forbidding portrait by Diane Arbus (I forget which), there might be incense that was all-too-sweetly thickening the air like jasmine jello, and the gauzy background music of rock violins…

The history of this specific lovers' googoo long preceded us. Tiny ceramic or lacquered containers, often described by unwitting or fastidious antique purveyors as snuff (or pomade or potpourri) holders, are boxes in which the worshipful swain would save, as tokens, corpses of the fleas he'd remove from his mistress's clefts and swells. This intimate grooming, for most of humankind at most points on the timeline, has been traditional, a natural result of, on the one hand, need for vehicles by which corporeal exploration could take place unashamedly—and, on the other hand, the age-old unstoppable day-and-night assault of sheer pestiferousness.

You put both hands together, and you have some satin-draped Renaissance dandy fondling away at a bosom made almost buttocky by its tight underlacing, tittering from both he and she, and pseudoscientific observations on the chessleap prowess of fleas beginning, by pucker and flush, to metamorphose into whatever version is current of "Oh, my little éclair cream…!" So, here: Cynthia and myself.

At moments like that (and remember: we were twenty, and lucky, and dumb) it seemed the hugest emotions we owned, the most gargantuan thoughts our brains could fashion (that is, what we felt toward each other, that limited range of ourselves we understood in those hazed-over days to be our whole existence) rose from deep inside us somewhere, bumping against the skin from underneath like whales about to breach. "Exhilarating" doesn't come close. "Here: you missed one." Then I'd be at The Source, transported, gobbling her up like crazy.

There is some evidence (and much popular belief) that fleas prefer a female's chemistry (*pulex*, "flea," may take its name from the Latin *puella*, "girl"). Be that as it may, the flea-trap has its own trivial place in the history of ladies' fashion. A German print shows one kind, worn as a pendant between the breasts. This trap is perforated throughout its columnar length with holes just right for a flea-sized shady siesta: inside, the flea encounters a gummy tube. Hung on a velvet ribbon, the trap is as pleasing a decoration as any. Strips of fur were also used. Lore even has it that lapdogs were selectively bred toward a similar purpose. Women carried long ivory sticks—again: this was an acceptable, public statement—for scratching the scalp from amidst the intricate palps and infoldings of their Marie Antoinette coiffures.

The link between fleas and female hormonal rounds is most amazingly seen in the life of that very excellent specialist, the European rabbit-flea. It clusters on the female rabbit, and only there—it would soon die in, say, the fur of a cat or the shag along a farm rat's groin—and, in the spring, up to seventy form a community on a single rabbit's ears, the place from which attempts to dislodge them are least efficacious. There they slurp and snooze and do whatever broad-jump acrobatics the space of a rabbit's ear allows.

Every stage in the rabbit-flea's cycle—ovulating, the ripening of eggs—is triggered by hormone cues in the host-doe's blood as *she* becomes pregnant, and then by the blood of her newborn litter, to which the fleas migrate for one frenzied spate of flea sex and the subsequent laying of eggs. The larvae from these will find the warren floor a rich profusion of food in the form of droppings; and then, of course, the young rabbits are there to eventually host the new flea generation. The timing of this, and its exquisitely fine-tuned dependence, is something to quicken your breath, like watching a vee of Canada geese turn *snap* on an airy dime as if it outlined a single sinuous manta ray… Except it's fleas we've got here, filth-colored repugnantly-ugly butt-blood suckers: fleas.

Was that interesting? While it was happening, we finished, in that moment twenty years ago: Cynthia, me. Then we lay wet and thoughtless, I was yakking probably out of nervousness, we both had residual energy and emotional hodgepodge itching under our skins, we were raw to the world's least touch, and each other's touch, *imagined* touches could rummage our psyches and pull strings taut there. What I said that did it, I don't remember; or what she said back. It might have been about that cat, a mean neurotic boneless beast at best—but that's a guess, and then I was an arrogant sonofabitch, and she was blind to her own intense Queen Termite spasms of laziness: all of the standard invective, razor-edged with intimate knowledge. We didn't fight fair; we were truthful.

And I wouldn't apologize: no.

In minutes, I was out walking the evening sidewalks of Ithaca, New York, the bile already starting to pit my tongue. It was dead-middle summer. Heat charmed out of the asphalt did snake-hulas in the air. The sky grew eggplant black, then flat black. When the moon showed, she was pitted too.

It had happened this quick: like a match to the gas. Like some one small word to our Big Talk. Whoosh.

On Monday, the 12th of October 1654, at 10:30 A.M., in the Dutch city of Delft, where both Vermeer and Leeuwenhoek were not only born in the same year (1632) but entered on the same page of the church baptismal records...a powder magazine exploded—*90,000* pounds of powder—killing untold hundreds and making wreck of the streets in a flash, so much so that, in the words of Elizabeth Stuart, Queen of Bohemia, who visited, "not one stone upon another" remained.

～

We might see the past as glorious in scale, either personally (before the Company failed, I was v. p. in charge of production...) or historically (the grandeur that was Rome, ah!...). And the same is true of the future: any nascent aspiration is projectable as grandiose.

But for the most part, when we extend ourselves through time it makes us smaller. Though it's *me*, it's not the me-who's-here-imagining-this-in-the-Present-Tense: I'm watching another "me," me-prime, recede through temporal distance as I'd watch a figure dwindle through distance in spatial terms. The blood-stuffed, psyche-whomping, undeniable Present Moment is the certainty, the survival-worthy; past and future slope from it on either side, forming a sort of equilateral triangle of perception, and the diminishing "me's" who fill it to fore and aft decrease appropriately to fit their respective far-offness.

Being a child again is smaller. Being very much older is smaller. If we retrojected ourselves to seventeenth-century Delft, retaining the integrity of a physical body, but having that body time-shrink by—let's see...350 years...we'd be about the size of a flea.

Say this one, at the base of the wall, near the little wood-case foot-warmer, in this room of the building that faces, on one side, the Voldersgracht and its whitewash-bricked Old Woman's and Old Man's Almshouse, which he'll also do, but now he's having Catherina unfasten the ties of her bonnet and let the sun trowel morning onto the pleats of her jacket he's going to get *so* right you can feel its lemon and burgundy nap in the paint.

(And the flea—? Oh, yes, we *could* be larger than that—but then we'd be correspondingly incorporeal. This is the choice that ghosts make.)

⌒

If we enter Delft through his *View of Delft*—if we enter into the picture plane, as light—we face the Schiedam Gate on the

Rotterdam Canal of the river Schie, from the south. The water is partly a dark, morocco brown from the last of the rain clouds, and from reflections cast by buildings on the farther bank. These buildings are themselves just coming into their own aged colors, now that the storm is passed. Beyond—and more buff, or celadon—the tower of the Nieuwe Kirk (where Vermeer was baptized) rises; and beyond that, even, we see—and where we can't, we sense—the colors of everyday human use, the salmon roof tiles and deep wine burgheress gowns and inlaid humidors of tobacco, divvying up the field of vision into its various commercial and domestic arrangements.

What we see here, then, is light in its first being shaped, from its even and definitionless travel, to being "sky"—this is "weather," the bunching mackerel-gray of the laden clouds, the emptier clouds a range of slightly soiled cotton, then the cloudless blues that shade off, near the roofline, to something almost white: a white that's been around.

And so, as we enter in, and down, we see light architectured, filling the empty lanes between buildings—so "building" bordered things, transparent structures of its own.

Now light is…*exemplified*, it's seven points on seven stacked apples, it's ringed in a puddle-top's ripples, it's flat, it's latticed by shadows, it's blinding.

And now it hits—no, it's so gentle I'd say it endorses—the side of a building, his building, and *some* of this light that says in representation *all* of this light, is softly entering the window that always admits light in his paintings, from the left side, onto a table like powder, crinkled over a wall-map in saurian folds, minutely flowering as many times as there are pearls in the necklace of pearls she's lifting…light, domesticated.

"Yes…so; with the strand like…yes…yes…Good!"

His wife is Catherina Bolnes. She is a remarkable woman, and will be for many years after her husband's death. By her decision to marry out of her religion and out of her approximate class (this Johannes Van der Meer is an innkeeper's son and the inn is a less than…um, *seemly* place), and by the little we know of her battles with debt in the years of her widowhood, we imagine someone of sharp-boned character, heedful of her own current. Yes, and by the nine paintings we now assume to be portraits of her, we look at a woman in whom the journey of light from the heart of the sun, through the atmosphere, onto the lace of the collar that wings her throat—is a culmination. "Like so?"

"*Fah!* You moved when you said 'Like so.'"

"But I should be like—this. You see?"

"No. Yes…Good! And undo the ties?" She's wearing one of those puffed white caps that look like conestoga wagon tops.

"So?"

"Yes. Good." Some paint. Long silence. "Still, now…still. You're beautiful, 'Thrina, it glints along your skin as if you were a guilder."

And next to *her,* Jan Vermeer loves his light. I say "his" light because this is what happens, somehow, at the sill of the world and house: the light that implicates the planet in all of its fullness, that marries the continents to the seas, becomes a personal field here, across the maps and globes of continents and seas he has in his work so often. "His" light. A solace of light.

Some paint. Long silence.

"*Ya!*"

"What! 'Thrina!"

Fussing at her waist.

"You moved. What?"

"One of the little devil-wanger imps is on me."

"Here" / sigh / "let me help with it."

at her bodice

You know what follows.

⁓

O flea, thou amorist!
Thou pepper grain that spicest us to our canoodling!

⁓

The poemlet often called "Fleas" (I believe it's anonymous; sometimes you find it billed as "the briefest poem in the English language"):

Adam
Had 'em.

places our prickler squarely at The Beginning: it was naked flesh
from the word "go." (Actually, fleas date from the Cretaceous,
when a two-winged ancestor scavenger-insect discovered that
blood was not only a nourishing swill, but high on the findability
scale; wings atrophied, legs grew resourcefully jumpworthy: this
was the proto-flea.) Goldbarth has written—addressing both the
antiquity and the ubiquity of this intimate relationship—an
"Addendum Couplet":

As did
Madam.

and pretty much prides himself on it.

⁓

There's a centuries-long salubrious tradition of flea as inciter to
carnal cha-cha-cha. Potential lovers frisk one another in search
of a barb-tipped interloper. Places best left unthought-of are

flea-tickled. Raiment becomes disarrayment. The rest is so many rut and estrus dominoes tumbling, slickety-slick. The flea as excuse, as Muse of Physical Passion. Fleas and brothels are commonly linked. We still say of somebody looking to nibble a bit of the ol' hot pastrami, looking to dip in a little tuna fondue, if you get my drift, that he or she "has the itch." The flea reminds even the clergy of what stuff's stuffed out of sight down there — its enlivening jig, from Eden onward, up and down out whozee-whatsis.

This same sly service is even performed for the gods of Olympus, in Willart de Grécourt's 16-page erotic poem *L'Origine des puces* — not a great poem, no, but equally engaging an origin story as that of Cretaceous mutation. Cupid, it turns out, is vexed when an ambrosia-lubricated convocation of the deities turns sleepy under Morpheus's intervening, instead of orgiastic. He shoots an arrow, the arrow turns into a swarm of fleas, and before you know it, divine thighs and mammaries undulate winsomely from divine togas, with three days and nights of mad coupling resulting. After which, the new insects are banished to Earth, and adapt to it beautifully.

"Fleas are so much a German erotic specialty," Brendan Lehane writes, "that two learned Teutons, Herren Hugo Hayn and Alfred N. Gotendorf, applied themselves at the turn of the century to compiling a bibliography of the literature. *Floh-Litteratur*, they called it," from the sixteenth century up. But the Germans have no monopoly here; and by the sixteenth century, something like the

> ...flea
> mankind one morning stared to see
> on Catherine Desroches' bared breast
> sucking imperturbably

is a well-established folk *motif de prurience*. A poem ascribed to Ovid has its narrator imagining he can—*poof*—become a flea at will, and so spelunk flesh grottoes. Long after, a character in Marlowe's *Faust* says, "I am like to Ovid's flea. I can creep into every corner of a wench." Lehane: "There is in fact a whole class of erotic flea art." Night: a candle: an off-white cambric shift uprumpled in search of some coven of spiky-snouted scoundrels, and there you have it: the two full moons and the fertile crescent, the nasties, the nougat, the grail.

An example of our lusty flea in the knowingmost of literary abilities would be, of course, Donne's poem, from when he was known, still, as "a great Visiter of Ladies, a great Frequenter of Plays, a great Writer of conceited Verses." This sexy, savvy paean to the gourmandizing flea as tiny armored-over "marriage temple" where (because "It suck'd me first, and now sucks thee") "our two bloods mingled bee" was (a Norton anthology says) "apparently the most popular of Donne's poems in his own century." Donne died in 1631; Leeuwenhoek was born the year after; "The Flea" was first published in 1633. A kind of flea Golden Age.

But if you've been waiting for gland-enflaming quotations from less-than-literary sources, if you really want to swag the haggis, down the banana cream pie, and scramble the sugar-eggs, if you get my drift and I think you do, *voilá*, from (purportedly) 1789 (but more likely a century later), the caviar, the crown, the catered lazy susan's topmost radish rosette of all flearotica (if you'll allow me the coinage), Anonymous's still-in-print spunk-spewing classic, *The Autobiography of a Flea*:

"Born I was—but how, when, or where I cannot say. I shall not stop to explain by what means I am possessed of human powers of thinking and observing, but, in my lucubrations, leave you simply to perceive that I possess them and wonder accordingly. My earliest recollections lead me back... I was engaged upon professional business connected with the plump white leg of a lady, the taste of whose delicious blood I well remember, and the flavour of whose —

"But I am digressing."

The lady is Bella, domicile, provender, and means of vast travel, all three sometimes at once, to our narrator; also an endless amusement:

"They have sat her upon the edge of the table, and one by one they sucked her young parts, rolling their hot tongues round and round in the moist slit. Bella lent herself to this with joy, and opened to the utmost her plump legs to gratify them…"

…and so on, for 190 pages in my paperback edition, while our *raconteur* himself is supposedly perched at the lip-edge of waterfall torrents, lumberjack fellings, Richter-scale seismic upquakings, and mud-slide inundations of human venality.

Thou nethermost peek up the vents of taboodom!

O flea, that bearest considerable great witness!

〜

And *we*
Can witness the *flea:*

〜

The *Talmud* knew: the flea, "being one of the animals that propagate by copulation, is therefore not to be killed on the Sabbath."

But this was an isolated knowledge. Pliny the Elder had said that "leapers" were "engendered by filth, acted upon by the rays of the sun," and straight from the Romans to the moment Leeuwenhoek pincered one up from a china jar to the gaze of his *dainty Lens*, the flea was a sexless creature, springing wholly grown into life through spontaneous generation. The flea's "Originall is from dust," wrote Thomas Moufet late in the sixteenth century, "chiefly that which is moyst'ned with mans or Goats urine." That a German engraving from 1749 shows two fleas mating in accurate detail, each brushy plate of her carapace holding its own knot of light, and he, in his underposition, credibly shadowed and textured with burls and jointwork...

...this can be traced exactly to that table in Delft, the morning sun backing his finicking wire tweezers, yes and his *enduring, unprejudiced Stare* . He writes, as if both declaring and winning the war in one compact statement, "Fleas are not produced from corruption, but in the ordinary way..."

~

Depending on how you mean "ordinary."

The penis of the male flea is the singlemost intricate penis known on the planet.

It consists of *two* rods, a thick and a thin, that twine about each other in his body caduceus-like. The sperm are wound like spaghetti around the thinner, longer shaft. When the two fated fleamates have found each other by whatever rarefied sense they use, crossing the Gobi and Tetons of our bodies; when he completes what Lehane endearingly dubs his "demurring zigzag" of wooing; and then when he's finally fitted beneath her, back to belly and tail to tail; THEN his rods uncoil, the thick rod snugged in a blind pouch halfway up her ample tract, the thin rod sliding in a groove along the thicker one, steadied thereby and directed, until it surpasses the thick rod, probes its way into her ultimate vaginal opening, yes and THERE it pushes its payload tangle of sperm and "somehow" releases it.

This takes maybe three hours, sometimes up to nine, and neither merrymaker halts feeding. All this while, the male is also using yet *another* organ, a kind of a feather duster with which he gently strokes his own true inamorata. Really.

Returning them gingerly into the blue china jar "…to set the Truth before my eyes, to embrace it, in order to draw the World away from Old-Heathenish superstition, to go over to the Truth, and to cleave unto it" even, yea, for this his "very minute and despised creature." Sliding the lenses' brass slips fussily back into their oxblood leather case. Time now for an ale with Vermeer, and trading tales of an honest morning's work. Let the tavern wits turn a few easy verses.

> A flea climbing out of my beverage
> Said "My wife is much taller than average.
> How can I keep her?
> I can't even leap her
> Without using one dick for leverage."

~

Okay, so Thomas Moufet was wrong about the ways fleas are engendered; so they *don't* scrabble *ex nihilo* from some log's mud-scabrous sides. But (in addition to being, as some claim, the father of *that* Miss Muffet, who comes through time to us with her fabled food and arachnophobia—plausibly so, in light of both the name and the father's interest) he was a man of learning "who," John Aubrey mentions, "hath written a Booke *De Insectis.*"

Moufet supplies us remedies for "the Torment" (including Dwarf Elder leaves, Fern root, Rue, and flowers of Pennyroyal); relates how the clever fox relieves itself of the pests (by mincing backwards into a river with a rag of moss in its teeth, until the ever-more-crowded fleas are on its snout, then just its nose, and then have no choice but to jump to what quickly becomes a moss raft floating downstream); and offers up quite a neat phrase when he wants to: of their biting, he says "they leave a red spot as a Trophie of their force."

He was one of an informal school of sixteenth-century men of letters shepherded over by Mary Herbert, Countess of Pembroke—Donne would be included here, as well as Edmund Spenser, Ben Jonson, and Thomas Nashe. She must have been an extraordinary person, "a beautiful Ladie and an excellent witt, and had the best breeding that age could afford"— it's Aubrey again. "She was a great Chymist," he tells us, with a "Laborator" to concoct in, and under her lithesome guidance "Wilton House was like a College, there were so many learned and ingeniose persons." She knew Sir Walter Raleigh. She toured with the Queen. She suggested her brother the poet Philip Sidney write his book *Arcadia*, which she revised and addended. Her own *bon mots* could be hurled in Greek, Latin, or Hebrew.

And this: "She was very salacious, and she had a Contrivance that in the Spring of the yeare, when the Stallions were to leape the Mares, they were to be brought before such a part of the house, where she had a *vidette* (a hole to peepe out at) to look on them and please herselfe with their Sport."

—Enormous wicked fun, to picture her leaning observantly into this pastime. Yes, but today I can only see Leeuwenhoek scribbling in front of me, blocking the view. I look over his shoulder: he's writing up notes on one more session spent with the flea, *endowed with as great Perfection in its kind as any large Animal*.

~

Fact: Its leap is *80 times* its length high, *150 times* its length long. This makes the frog or the kangaroo seem anemic younger cousins.

Fact: The fleabite isn't a bite. It's a piercing and siphoning up. The responsible tool is made up of three stiletto-shaped blades—and good blades, so sharp the pierced skin doesn't relay it.

Fact: It's not this piercing that causes the itch, but enzymes in the flea's saliva, which enters the wound in a forceful injection and keeps the bloodflow from coagulating. Now the flea imbibes—for many hours, if undetected. It will suck more blood than its body can bear, and the excess spurts straight out its anus.

Fact: There are 2,000-plus flea species.

Fact: 932 hedgehog-fleas have been found on a single young hedgehog.

Fact: But monkeys *aren't* natural hosts to fleas. The picking we see is to clear their own packed, gummy body-scurf. They can, however, accidentally catch human-fleas from zoogoers.

Fact: I said the human-flea, *our* flea, *Pulex irritans*: "irritating flea." The name is lived up to.

Fact: The patient pupal flea in its case will wait alive but inactive, over a year, for a proper host to appear. It *knows*. A realtor unlocking a house abandoned for months, in which not one free flea has been leaping, can walk right through and briskly out the back door, and emerge with 150 crisscrossing snappily under his pants.

Fact: Almost everybody. Everywhere.

Fact: Every three days the priests of ancient Egypt shaved their heads (this, from Herodotus) specifically to keep their scalps flea-free. And still they scratched.

Fact: Indian noblemen had themselves hoisted dandily off the floor at night, in light cane hammocks that were dangled from the roof (according to Marco Polo) specifically to ward off the flea. And still they scratched.

Fact: A wardrobe from the court of Henry VIII was discovered, and spilling from the tucks of its clothes was a dry pour of the bodies of mummified sixteenth-century fleas. Kings scratched. Queens scratched. Viziers and flouncing extramarital favorites scratched, and scratched.

Fact: Jesus the Christ scratched fleas.

Supposition: They were, then, the first to take the "host" of Mass; the only to take it directly.

Fact: The Buddha scratched fleas.

Fact: Mohammed scratched fleas.

Fact. Cleopatra, only an hour after bathing in asses' milk and rose-petals, having had a handmaiden lotion her, then a eunuch strigil the lotion off…Cleopatra scratched fleas. The handmaiden scratched. The eunuch.

Fact: With his head in The World of Original Forms That Precede All Earthly Existence, Plato dug into his tummy. Thinking radium, Madame Curie rubbed an ankle abstractedly with an ankle. Then went at it good, with a pen nib. Isadora Duncan. The Czar. The Continental Congress. Scratched.

Fact: At the Barrel-and-Boar in Delft, with one proper citizen's one proper ale before him, waiting Vermeer's appearance, Leeuwenhoek (drawing a crazed but clear distinction between his cozy colony of fleas in the china jar—that is, his objects *of dear Contemplation*—and any sybaritic invader profaning the sanctum-space of his body—that is, *Vermin*) scratched a fine ten-fingered tarantella all over his butt. And fifty-six years later, his British disciple Henry Baker ("on whom seems to have fallen," says one biographical note, "the Dutch microscopist's mantle") scratched. When Baker met Daniel Defoe in 1727, Defoe was scratching. Two years later, Baker married young Sophia Defoe; the preacher, two fiddlers, and every flower-bounteous maid in the wedding party, was witnessed, off and on for that entire grand evening, scratching.

There was also the scratch of Defoe's quill pen. In 1722, in the room where his paper-tumulted desk moved into afternoon with morning light still tenaciously dabbed across it…Defoe is writing a fiction—though founded on fact.

Defoe is writing *A Journal of the Plague Year*.

⌒

"Then, came such a Stink upon the wind; from the bodies piled at corners in wait of the Dead Carts making their rounds; and from a City tormented by running Sores; and from the market goods and the rubbish heaps and the stores of grain and salted cuts that had, from the terrible toll of the labourers, none to attend them; and so they rotted; the Stench being such, the saying was this: the Air was of a thickness, you could climb it as if it were a ladder; each new death, being a rung.

"A girl, a Hooper's daughter, she not above Six years of age; her father and mother having exhibited the Tokens over their chests and arms, and Expiring, both, within the same night, to the grief of an older son, who fled the City on foot, and no one has heard to this day; then the girl, when she exhibited Tokens, *viz*, the black swellings, there was none who would go near, and so she wandered the Parish for two nights sleeping in rain and all. I saw of her next on Joiner Street where it meets the earthen wall, she had swooned. And then I saw her pitiful body in Spasms, ogglddypoggldy, as if dancing or thrown about; at which her Chest bled; and at the bleeding her skin did break; and out crawls a Rat with her spleen in its jaws yet. This was the cause of her being worked from the inside like a Judy puppet. And I would fall weeping right there, save for a nasty pack of the creatures were all upon her then, with their devilish piping that squeals right through like a knife. And the morning next, she was bones."

⌒

It begins: in the blood of marmots and susliks among the steppes of central and eastern Asia. And there the disease is mild (as syphilis was, in New World systems, before Columbus's men introduced it to Europe). In times of migration, however, these rodents mingle with countryside rats. Some fleas, by mistake or intent, transfer over; and with them, as in a decanter, come the bacilli.

Rats die then; some, not all. Of the surviving, some of these open-air rats will eventually come to share their fleas with the rats at the edges of cities: and here, a new player enters onstage.

For when a rat dies and its carcass cools, its population of fleas will seek a living rat; and if none is easily found, as can happen when rats by the thousands are toppling over foaming, an alternative is available. Without even trying, the horror has made its way to the top of the corporate ladder.

We first read of plague in *Samuel*, Book 1, Chapter V: as punishment for stealing the Ark of the Covenant, the Philistines are smote. The populations of Gath, Ashod, and Akron: smote. First documentation, in an historical sense, is from the pandemic that decimated Justinian's Rome, beginning 542 A.D. At the height of that misery 10,000 people a day were dying, filling the air with cries and stinks we can't begin to imagine without touching madness and so we back off. This outbreak lasted sixty years, and pushed its fatal reach "to the ends of the habitable world." At its finish, the Dark Ages start.

"And a mother was dead, but the child still crawled her breast; and sucked most piteously there; to no avail, save a trickle of Rheum; and tho the child was plucked away and bathed of its Contagions, it was purple in a night; and this scene we were obliged to witness daily; until an infant was a purse of weeviled meal you heaved across your shoulder into a Pile; and called upon the Constable to shovel them into a Pit."

Lulled down to occasional, local swaths of tragedy over the centuries, plague as a pandemic reemerges with fatalities among a host of Tartars who, in 1346, besieged a colony of Italians at

Caffa, a trading town in the Crimea. At no great loss for martial efficiency, Tartar war chiefs ordered their own dead catapulted over the city walls. When the siege was relieved, and the extant Italians homed again in Genoa, it was only a matter of days —a matter of fleas in half-inch switches of host and hostess—and the infamous Black Death had started gnawing away at the succulent ribmeat of Europe. Even Greenland was tortured. In three years, a quarter of Europe was dead; in less than twenty years, half.

Survivors, for as long as they remained survivors, thought it was the end of the world—and in a sense they were right. One out of every two: marked with the pustules, the cold sweats, retching, then dead. This surge lasted 300 years, its farewell performance being the Plague of 1665 Defoe writes so movingly of—100,000 Londoners were added, as a last flash, to the utter devastation. You slept beside Death, and you woke facing Death, and you caroused or fasted in excess with Death's breath on the x between your shoulders, pontiff or shitpicker, harlot or saint. "And now the Wagons, that they sent by once a day for the dead; they sent by twice; and this was not sufficient, the dead would tumble from their stacks and land in the Streets cracked open; and none would go near, for fear of what issued; no, not even a dog."

The Great Fire of London one year later burnt five-sixths of the city—having, perhaps, as much as anything else to do with quieting the plague. Again it existed as only a fitful flicker for centuries—a rumor here, a measley 30,000 Cairoese there, a wink, a nibble. Then in January 1894 a woman in Canton fell ill. It arrived in Hong Kong and passed to Bombay—and from that city's trading vessels the third great plague pandemic spread worldwide; the most savage: *thirteen million* people dying in a calamitous heap on the steps of the twentieth century.

All this while, no one suspected the flea. (It took until 1910 for the Plague Research Commission to pinpoint the culprit.)

They burnt Jews instead. In London, in 1665, 200,000 cats and 40,000 dogs were killed, as a precaution. Some wore large dried toads as amulets. Tar was poured onto fires, to cleanse the air of its "Poisons." Coins and letters were dipped in vinegar, or handled by cups on long rods. Pepys carried a hare's foot. They burnt Arabs. They severed the heads of the poor. Jackdaws and pigeons were trapped and given over to the knife in unimaginable numbers. That the flea was never efficaciously suspect, not in 1,400 years, is testimony, of a silent but eloquent sort, to its acceptance as a fact of life. You breathed, you shat, your soul hearkened unto the Throne of the Lord, your groin was aburble with longing, the sun shone, it hailed, and you had fleas.

"And some were of an Opinion, the wind did bear it; and these would show themselves only if clothed in a cloak and gloves of cloth and a Mummer's mask; and some of the Opinion, it abided in the waters; and these drank naught, or these drank Spirits only; and some said God above; and some said Satan below; and none knew, save for this, that its Conveyance to the Humours of the body was of a common Particular, not to be avoided (withal through Chance); and in those days a man would not so much as rub his own two hands for warmth or scratch his own Fleas or with his knuckles dig the sleep out from his eyes; without prayer; or a Shudder."

~

O flea, thou Carrier, thou millionth-gram of Oblivion.
Thou scourge, thou Humbler, thou Totterer of Goliaths.
Thou Pygmy with poison-tip dart.
Thou Death Speck, thou dillseed Accessory to the Crime.
Woe dot. Destroyer.

~

So I apologized.

This story's this simple: the tiniest units that introduce love, conduct huge suffering. Lollapalooza hurt lives on this planet, people. No one's exempt. Why add more hurt or turn from one of the little, saving annealing-moments we're given?

Besides, I was lonely, more lonely than proud; and she was breathing out there somewhere with those freckles paprika'd over her nose, and her barrister's manner of nailing a tough question home, and that amberthatched snickerdoodle between her legs that enjoyed my own gargoyley thing. Whatever pushed me over—a crash at the corner, a classmate's leukemia, Alan's parents' divorce, or maybe I was up reading about the plague one night for a history course that told me history's never finished with us, history's ever-voracious…I was knocking on Cynthia's door. I knew we didn't need to keep on garnishing Pain with our own small sprigs of Petulance.

No dummy, I'd brought a peace gift: this, a small ceramic lozenge case I claimed was one of those antique token-boxes in which the lovestruck swain collected his mistress's nimble leapers…oh, I was golden-tongued. I thought it might be an easy key back to our former intimacy, and also a way of saying (though not in words) how I accepted the place of that prissy, pissy, parasite-smuggling cat in her life and mine. No dummy, she took the case with a calculated aloofness, and required of us a gauntlet of conversational reassurances and proofs, before we were once again nuzzling each other across her sheets, her lips a remora on me, mine improvising red-hot jazz on her chickfuzz ocarina.

Now that was all so long ago, it shrinks to a postcard scene— its grandiose romance and randy rollaround are…"quaint," I suppose: what twenty years does. And yet the substance scrib-bled on that postcard's back is true, is simple but true, and I've brought you through all of this pop-historical voyeuristic pseudo-memoir Oompahpah-and-Fizz to share it:

The transmitter's size says nothing about the total jolt of the message: what *are* we if not the exquisite parquetrywork of chromosomes, retarded or voluptuous by assignment of perhaps a single gene? Oh nodes no larger than peas can double us over, and these are the casters on which well-being wheels. One scant nodded *yes* or stuttered *no* will drive an entire life from its route. We need to be attentive, to the smallest rising moon above a cuti-cle, to the lilliput taj mahal of blue at the center of any red flame, to the slimmest syllable love or politics utters, yes and because our forgiveness is the flimsiest mote in the galaxy's eye and our tenderness as well, we need to practice them daily, turn to some-one who matters and practice them daily, as if repetition does count, for suffering's armory of small but endless plague-marks adds a grief to a grief and finally strikes with the strength of a huge blunt instrument, and even the least of our comforts and dignities needs to be archived, kept well-lubed and, when required, mar-shaled in attempt to be a counterbalancing force.

A stranger, some punk twenty-year-old imposter claiming my name, has sent this sentiment to me over two decades of daily fuss and kaboom, and I think I'll hearken.

He'll know Cynthia for a year more maybe, tops. She'll go to law school, then on to Japan. The squabbles won't stop with this single apologetic tryst. But for the moment, as I unwind time and see him, he's stroking her shoulders while she dozes, he's coming to see (not that the wisdom will always remain with him when it's needed, no, but nonetheless coming to see) we need to care about each other down to units the size of just one umber asexual freckle...stroking her, thinking this, idly with his other hand jiggling the little case that he bought—because he's clever, you see—at a flea market.

Cynthia's deep, damp breaths...the cat in its psycho slumber...

He looks up at, and into, her poster of the painting of Delft. One spark, no one knows whose or how, and the top of that city was blown off like a skull from a .45 at the palate. Although it's rebuilt by the time Vermeer immortalizes his view across the river, the mackerel grays that float above the water, the rich clay colors roofing the farther plane...

If he could ray himself to a point, he'd be of size enough to wander those backmost Delftways, past the peculiarly whitewashed jambs of that time and place, and find the Barrel-and-Boar. Vermeer has just entered. Leeuwenhoek raises his long-emptied mug in halloo.

"Hoofdman!"

~

By the time of his death, Jan Van der Meer—Vermeer—will have fathered eleven children (eight of them still minors when he dies).

No wonder he sometimes itches sorely to vamoose, breathe-in the outside, slant a flagon with the guys. (We hope Catherina escapes sometimes as well, an empty wicker basket over her arm, and nothing but giddiness guiding her, maybe down the wharf steps, to Van Loo's, where bolts of goldshot damask are being unrolled on a large dry tarp, and sun picks over the gold like lute strings, yes... But today is Vermeer's.)

From what we know, it's likely he succeeded his father as the innkeeper of the Mechelen, a tipple-spot off the market square at the corner of Oudemanhuisteeg; he and Catherina would have lived in its two upper floors. So it won't do, of course. The morning's paints are drying, what he wants for some few minutes is *away*.

"*Hoofdman!*" says Leeuwenhoek on seeing him enter the tavern dimness, and raises his empty mug as if a second round might rain into it from the rafters. ("Head man," is what it means, a bigwig in the Artist's Guild: as if a friend might yell "Yo, Prez!" or "Heydeeho it's Boss Man!") Soon enough, the seventeenth-century Netherlands bullshit is batted back and forth.

"My friend"— this is three rounds later—"the shell of the beetle I have been studying under my little glass…it looks exactly like a *viola da gamba!*" He makes the shape in the air.

"Then it must look exactly like Gjerta there," and Vermeer nods near-imperceptibly toward the tavernmaid they like and tease, the way they like and tease each other; he makes the same shape back in the air, for Leeuwenhoek. "My dear shepherd of beetles, you've been too long with your eye at your device."

"*Faa!* You've been too long with your eye drilling over to Gjerta. You could muddy her pee, your looking is so intense. Eleven's enough!" (The seventeenth-century test for pregnancy was clarity of the urine.)

"And from your bees and beetles you've learned to sneak those little conscienceful stings of yours into a conversation. But listen, now: my *mission* is looking. Yes, and looking *impartially*"— he gestures like a balance-pans—"on the pitying face of the Virgin Herself above the font in the nave, and on the lovely plumpness peeking from Gjerta's lacings."

"*You*, look? Jan, stare out the door, at the light there. What do you see?"

"Oh, go fish with your nose in your beer."

"No, truly: What?"

"You can see it yourself. There's Houckgeest's shop. The

entrance to his side lane. The front stoop. Way in back, the roofs of the street where Steen's bakery is."

"Jan… The light is filled with dancing motes. Look. They dazzle, then they turn the other cheek like a good dour Christian, then they flare up again. There are thousands and thousands"—he drifts his hand from front door to kitchen door—"floating in here across your chin and your dingus, man, into the shadows, all over!"

"And you could spend the afternoon counting the dancing last of them, and not see that the shaft of light you're looking straight into pours like a, a, bath of apricot brandy, over some sumptuous Gjerta or other."

"No, listen…"

Etc. You get the idea. Two friends, a few hours. The nubbling of extra texture into the breath-thin lining of life.

～

And *did* they know each other? That baptism record places them on the same page. Leeuwenhoek served well as the executor of Vermeer's (bankrupt) estate, and spent enormous energy satisfying its creditors. (This, though, might be an ordinary result of Leeuwenhoek's station in Delft burgher life at the time, as opposed to the role of longstanding family friend.) Between those parentheses Birth and Dying, the history is uncertain; experts argue differing likelihoods.

But we know Vermeer's father owned a silk-weaving business the son inherited; Leeuwenhoek was, by profession, a draper. And, writing of "Vermeer's change in style," one art historian says it "happens to coincide with Leeuwenhoek's return to Delft from Amsterdam."

Around that time, Vermeer evidently found the lenses and know-how for constructing a *camera obscura*. "The significant shift in both style and execution," says Leonard J. Slatkes, "is signaled by the *Soldier and Laughing Girl*." The effects "preserve the optical phenomena not visible to the naked eye but clearly observable in *camera obscura* images. Vermeer's unique application of paint in small dots, or *pointilles*, also seems to be an attempt to capture the specific visual qualities of the *camera obscura* projected image. Indeed, he seems to be the only painter who attempted this."

Shimmerings over the bread of *The Milk Maid*, over the side of the boats and bridge of the *View of Delft*, like so many diatom-tiny florins and stuyvers poured out of sunlight itself...these dots. And Leeuwenhoek, parsing his eyesight ever more rarefied, down to what he terms the "gloubles" that add up to living.

I think it was more than one day of ale they shared. I like to see it this way:

The light from what we call the universe enters Vermeer's open window—on the level of light, it must be like a needle threaded.

The painter humanizes—*familiarizes*—this unthinkably cosmic presence. Light is given its holdable, credible bodies here: it's curlicued impasto in the picture frames, and stippled over an ermine collar, and wrinkled with geology across the faces of wall-hung maps, it's clabbered here, it's seamlessly creamy there, it's alive, we can lift it, it's something the size of a pearl on a vanity table, glowing from the grain heart of a pearl...

And at the far end of that room it reaches Leeuwenhoek. He's absorbed in his peering. He's funneling that light to a pinpoint, to an as-yet-never-imagined pinpoint—where it burnishes, and turns like a bright star inside of, the jet back-case of a flea.

And so they make a two-man-unit engine of increasingly finer-focused resolution and power.

We need to be attentive.

⌒

/There's a submicroscopic level where color doesn't exist—the wavelengths of light are larger than any possible place to land.

/According to Frederick Turner's study, "The length of the human present moment"—the "bundles" of sensory intake by which our day is divided—is roughly three seconds. Basic units of meter, worldwide, are three seconds in reciting; conversational speech occurs in three-second bursts with milliseconds between; a listener takes in three seconds of speech at a time, to his processing centers. Below that, time in some real sense doesn't occur. Sounds separated by anything less than three-thousandths of a second are "heard" as simultaneous.

/God's seed in Mary. Christ in the wafer. Incubus. Succubus. Mercury visiting man in the guise of a peddler...

These are all from the realm of nonperception. Before Columbus, the map of a flat Earth drew a clear border between this realm and the known.

We might say the flea is that border, our last clear datum before we slip over into silence between black holes, electron spin, quark iffiness...

We might say the flea is the Edge of the World.

⌒

Well, we live in *this* world. C., not two years old, went in this week to have her chest sawed open. N., just twenty-two, jumped twenty-two stories and then his father was brought to identify what they bucketed. On the other hand, my sister calls, and she and Boog and the kids are fine, and the dog is fine, and the lawn is fine; she's hanging up now and sifting with him pollen by pollen into her fine sleep...

If they mean anything at the last, these fleas, it's because they say us, for us, while we're busy under the eddying fires of galaxies, under mountains-diminishing Big Bang pulses of time, pretending we're pretty large stuff.

They don't say the whole poignant nuanceful range, but I hope I've implied they have (or we impart to them) the basics down pat: our grief, and our cleaving unto another. When we forget, they remind us.

—Best, perhaps, at that nowadays-nearly-defunct, but idiosyncratic, crackpot institution-of-sorts, the flea circus.

Thomas Moufet tells us of "Mark an Englishman (most skilfull in all curious work)" who created a chain of gold, with key and lock to match, for shackling a flea, which then "did draw a Coach of Gold that was every way perfect." Indeed, as a formal idea the flea circus seems to have come from sixteenth-century England.

It has its geniuses.

Flamboyant ***Signor Bertolotto*** who, in the 1830s, "*Under the Patronage of Her Royal Highness the Princess Augusta*," included, as part of his Regent Street Flea Circus in the Cosmorama Rooms, a costumed twelve-piece flea orchestra "playing audible music"; he knew his fleas by individual name, and some of his most distinguished performers were, he let out, prolifically fed in secret by various "ladies of distinction."

Professor Leroy Heckler of Hubert's Freak Museum at Broadway and 42nd, a friend to the photographer Diane Arbus. She would finish midnight shoots of Congo the Jungle Creep, the Serpent Lady, Sealo the Seal Boy, midgets, pinheads, the chafing folds of the Fat Lady, Rudolf the Armless Man who used his toes to light his cigarette, Presto the fire Eater, Albert Alberta half-man half-woman... Then, with the living trash of that neighborhood starting its wee-hours rounds in the alleys outside, she'd recompose herself while Heckler fed his *artistes*. "He'd roll up his sleeves and, using tweezers, pick up the fleas out of their mother-of-pearl boxes, drop them on his forearm, and let them eat while he read the *Daily News*."

Professor Len Tomlin struggling impresario of (in 1974, at least) "Britain's one remaining flea circus," "POSITIFLEA AN ALL LIVE SHOW"—at that time he'd brought thirty years of dedicated flea ringmastership to his craft. "Only three men in the world," he is reported as saying, "have the steadiness of eye and hand to harness fleas."

And there are the Flea Stars leaping through circus history, too: for instance, Paddy, who "was said by Mr. Heckler to have given 52,850 consecutive performances, a record scientists say is quite impossible but which Mr. Heckler liked to call 'Broadway's longest run.'" Or the star of Copenhagen's Tivoli Gardens flea circus, "caught by a dowager countess in one of the city's most exclusive districts." In keeping true to its exquisite origins, this performer (a "tightrope dancer") was attired completely in pink, its costume fashioned from the down of one of the Copenhagen zoo's pedigreed flamingos.

Locked into roles we've decreed, they act out their rough parodies of our human passions—what I called "our grief, and our cleaving unto another." Gala battles are common, with uniformed ranks of flea foot soldiers (some bayoneted or dragging cannons) and stalwart generals leading them onward to carnage—Washington, Grant, Napoleon, all swords-drawn, astride flea chargers. There are pugilists and dueling fencers. Maidens are tied by villains to flea-sized railroad tracks and wriggle there most piteously. There is wailing and gnashing of teeth.

And there are the lovers. Romeo, rapt in the garden, courting a balconied Juliet; and then, with a single bounce, he's at her side. There have been elaborate flea weddings, down to the veil and bouquet. Flea waltzers, cheek to cheek. Fleas side-by-side in their own flea Tunnel of Love car. And, when the children and ladies are ushered out of the tent, gents, how'dja like to witness the Absolutely Sensational (but Educational) Spasms of Fourposter Prowess on the Honeymoon Night...

⁓

He covers her freckled shoulders with the sheet. Her breathing is deep and steady, it seems it must be in tune with something enormous, something as imperturbably confident as the Ithaca night sky itself. But he can't sleep one eyelash-worth of it. The dregs of sex are in him, I guess, or maybe some foreboding—who knows? I love him as I might a close friend's child. And it's so long ago...two decades shrinks this in size to one of those crystal globes you shake and it's snowing.

I shake it: he's holding her lightly now, the summer heat is woozying his wakefulness, he's staring through blur at the thumbtacked Vermeer, and he sees that it's snowing in Delft right now. A calm white hand is stroking the brows of its houses...

⁓

Usually the weather is clement. Oh, it can get cold—that corpulency we attribute to the figures in Dutch paintings, portly burghers and their dumpling wives, may partly be the up-to-seven-layers of underskirting and pants they wore. But real snow is rare. So Leeuwenhoek wants to study it, Leeuwenhoek's out in it, flumping through great white loaves. And it's quiet. It softens all detail. He can use a little of that.

Because eight minors is a lot of confusion for any dead man to have left behind, and especially a poor one. And all of the documents 'Thrina needs to sort through now, the many paper cogs of the many paper machines of this world...! So much. He wishes Jan could be here if just to complain about it.

Even so, he's watching each individual flake in its glide—he's Leeuwenhoek. He's seeing each unduplicated face in the choir, each separate star of descent—and then he's looking into distance, a landscape of simple enamel-white lengths.

He thinks, "These little ones!" Some must be in his eyes now, on his cheeks, they're damp. "These little ones, *ay-yi*, how they add up!"

The History of the Universe is Important to this Story

I.

$\mathcal{A}$nother woman. A *shiksa*. Though how Lucille Maxine Mandelbaum, the mother of my best friend Noschel Mandelbaum, discovered and was sure her husband Itzie "The Discount Siding and Paint Prince" Mandelbaum was *shtupping* some bottle-blonde bimbo-of-his-heart on the side, she could never explain exactly. She "just knew." There was "something." The science of wifely calculation "told her." Noschel and I understood: exquisite vapors foreign to a fourteen-year-old's cosmos permeated the air of 1962 and carried densely-textured, grievous information. We never doubted this.

And eventually the bimbo herself (yes, blonde; but reserved: a woman of great integrity and tenderness, as it turned out) made her role in the drama public. We were in college by then. Noschel was paged from the middle of Astronomy 101 to calm his mother—or was it his father?—at the height of their familial fracas. I have a recollection of clumsily following him from the lecture hall. (In every course we could, we sat together, self-paired as surely as if by skin-at-the-sternum from birth.) There's lots of excited talking that uses our hands, and the term "conniption fit" over and over.

It pretty much fizzles after that. Disclosures, lawyers: the usual. Nobody won. The neighborhood by then had fresher, fattier gossip to chew. And I had problems for the first time in my life that were my own, apart from any of Noschel's obsessions, and I think I took a very young man's pleasure in that independence, although the confusions of first-time sex and the edged woe of watching my mother grow weaker daily (from the "growth," as they called it, something as mad for territory as any warrior-king in the pages of freshman History)—these were uneasy pleasures, guilty ones. Maybe this was my initial whiff of those sorely laden vapors that informed and tormented the grownups' world.

Ah, but the special texture of those earlier four years!—when I would visit the Mandelbaums nightly, and Noschel and I would pick continuously at this magical family sore (was it *true*? how *could* he? what did *she* feel?), not so much like picking away at a scab, no, any two over-sheltered teenagers could do that, but this was more like creating scab on scab, a sculpture of scab, a plain of imposing scab Rushmores!

Of Itzie the blundering bigamist I have only the vaguest memories, but I remember he seemed like no particular villain the comic books or movies had ever displayed for me. I hear his complaining—business, fallen arches, business—but genially, and once he showed me a magic trick with a nickel. I see his sad black child's paintbrush of a moustache. The voice is immigrant-background Chicago Jew—blunt, clumping, eager to please—and the moustache swells and deflates as his upper lip plays with a bubble of air when he's frustrated. That's about all.

But Lucille I can still see as if twenty-seven years gone by were the width of a room in their gewgaw'ed-up apartment. When Noschel and I were six, she was shivering our scalps with Old World tales of Rabbi Loew, "this was in Prague, but you don't know from Prague, a city where the streets are twisted," and in his people's darkest hour he made an artificial man, the Golem, "a monster, a Frankenstein I'll tell you, only *good*," the Jews' defender, hunched in shadow at the side of an ale-house or a tannery, ready to leap for a throat... This seemed so strange an incarnation of justice; in school, it was an elegant robed woman holding a balance-pans.

"That Itzie, he's a monster," she once sighed as if we weren't there. Her hair was gold, but tired gold, and fisted into a bun that rode the top of her head like a sleeping gerbil; Noschel kept its counterpart, Kong, in a glass case in his bedroom. I was fourteen, I remembered her stories. Was I supposed to see Itzie now, that chicken-chested man, as a shambling cinema creature, bolts through his neck, a sewn gash round his forehead like a football's stitches, slobbering, shuffling cumbrously about? Though even then, I knew people were capable of damage larger than they were.

Noschel's fancies, once the bimbo had been hinted at, grew increasingly complex, and it was easy for the susceptible person I was back then to lose himself in the clouds of Noschel's preoccupation. Why not? The surface unruffleability of the grownup world, a given, had been sharply taken back: the Discount Paint Prince lived by other, secret laws. And we'd extrapolate, with tireless zeal, the other, secret world those laws implied.

"Does he, you know?" "What?" "You know." "No." "*No* what? *No*, you don't know; or *no,* he doesn't?" "Doesn't WHAT?" We're in his room, of course with the door closed and a sandpail-clothes-hanger-pile-of-pop-cans warning device attached to its knob. The gerbil, as usual, snoozes. I'd seen sandwich lunchmeat livelier than Kong. "SCREW her, you idiot!" It hurts, he has such energy behind the word. And then—as any mention of the flesh did, in those days—we're giggling.

Or: how did Itzie, who seemed to barely find time to let his breath wheeze out, squeeze such expansive, bacchanalian philandering into his fallen-arches-and-business-beset days? There was a comic book hero we all read then named Captain Invincible. One stupid neighborhood kids-joke went, "Well if he's invincible, how come you can *see* him?" I mention this because it was the favoritemost of Noschel's fantasy explanations in those early days: that Itzie invented Invisible Paint for the *shiksa*, and she actually lived right there in the apartment with them. "She watches him sleep with my mother." "You're crazy." "Maybe she's in my room right now." "Yeah? Squeeze her tits." Then we're giggling.

But the ultimate compulsion, of the later days, arrived with the rumor the bimbo had had a child by Itzie. A child almost our age. This half-brother ("brother," he quickly became in Noschel's determined largesse) was soon enough using up all of my friend's vast powers for detailing alternate worlds. My own delight remained in having some excuse for hypothesizing the mystery of adults' sex, in the loose range exalting-to-steamy. But the next two years intensified the brother's place in Noschel's cosmology, filling Noschel with hope, and terror. Neither of us had siblings— then this came along. It was no game. Cap, we called the brother, in some shaky connection to he of the stalwart moniker Invincible. Cap this, Cap that. We couldn't see him, but he was there all the time.

Cap was a thug, with two teeth gone, one gold, and time racked up in the slammer. Cap was a nuclear physicist. Cap was on TV, but used a fake TV name, like Brick or Shelby. Cap had a mil-

lion dollars, a *billion* dollars, and flew his own fighter plane. When
Cap and Noschel passed, an instant seismographic shock of hush-
hush brotherly recognition would rattle their bones. They'd *know*.
They each bore one half of a chromosomal tattoo that was drawing them—even now, irresistibly—together. Etc. Then, I
wouldn't admit it, but now I can see: I was jealous of Cap. "Some
brother—you make him up out of fart gas." This was an early
sign of my eloquence.

We'd bicker. Little things: favorite T.V. shows, baseball scores,
the size and desirability of Marsha Glickman's bazoomers. Really,
though, we were arguing Cap. The kids around us were building
credible smalltime empires out of stolen car parts; or were busy
assembling plastic true-to-scale aircraft carriers out of a thousand
pieces not much larger than rods and cones on the retina; or were
learning the rubber cement that came in those model kits was
a cheap high, and they'd sniff the gelid gobbets until they wafted
like smoke to the ceilings of their garages... There were Noschel
and I, squabbling in our sixteen-and seventeen-year-olds' parrot
voices over, say, Cap's middle name.

It bonded us, more than separated. Things changed after our
first year in college—I'll talk about that in a while. But when I look
back now to Astronomy 101 that day...

A lecture hall. The start of the semester, and Philolaus *(born
circa 480 B.C.)* is flat on his back in the toe-tip of Italy, watching
the night sky, thinking for all of us, theorizing a system that (before Copernicus!) moves Earth from its centerpoint in the universe.

That's what's diagrammed on the board—Philolaus's "Central
Fire" and, around it, in evenly-spaced concentric circles: the sun,
the moon, the Earth, the five other planets, the distant black
ring where the stars are permanent fittings, and (because that
totals nine and the Perfect Number is ten) another planet,

"Counter-Earth," he posits hidden from us on the opposite side of the "Central Fire."

Quite a convoluted use of Professor Schaumley's (or Schuster's? or Shumberg's?) chalk, and even so... A messenger from the Dean's high sanctum sidles politely in... There are whisperings, Noschel is called to the hallway, I follow...

And all of the planets hurtling through space at their planet-speed dwindle to dotted swiss on the frock I always imagine the bimbo is wearing before she slips out of it.

2.

But the history of the universe is important to this story.

It begins for my purpose with Philolaus, and ends for my purpose with Sir William Herschel wandering numb with discovery in the mazy afternoon light of his garden. He was the cutoff point of Astronomy 101, and backwards from him trailed a parade of skystruck men and occasional women who, in dogged purpose and eccentricity, had no peers (not even Arnie Fleischer, who could force a thread-thin gust of air from the corner of his right eye, and sat in the cafeteria shadows practicing nuances of this singular talent all through that autumn of 1966).

But for now, my purpose brings us to Castle Benatek, sometimes Benatky. The year is 1600. The season is autumn, air so clear you'd think the stars floated in from a granary up the way. The scene is the great flame-lit stone cooking-hall of Benatek, and there the air is greasy broth. Around the huge free-standing flagstone pillar of a hearth in the center, a huge free-stumbling pillar of a man is chasing another. (More on that other, in a moment.) The first, the fleshy Danish cave-bear of a man with the flaxen mustachios and a sloshing tankard roughly the size of a chamber pot in one gestures-flourishing hand—this is Tycho

Brahe, the Emperor Rudolph's personal mathematician and astrologer, and contestably the most honored skyscanner alive in his time. His other hand, as he lurches his circles, keeps making a grasping motion.

"Give the calculations here!"

"No!"—for his quarry is only half that drunk, and has a scant man's nimbleness as he skitters around the hearth.

"You pale homunculus, you lanky shanky spare-rib, give here!"

But the spare-rib will not, he crabs those scraps of paper ever closer to his chest.

"You dyspeptic-arsed tatterdemalion, give here!"

"No!"

"Gimme!" (or Danish to that effect).

"No way!" (or German to that effect).

And then a circling banner of curses in Latin from both of them.

About Tycho Brahe: the classroom facts. That he was born alive, a twin, in 1546—the brother stillborn. That at age one he was kidnapped by his childless uncle Jörgen: his childless, wealthy uncle Jörgen. That the boy was raised to privilege ("horses, dogs, and luxury," he summed it up) and a future of vaguely aristocratic service to the state. (His father's Helsingborg Castle, in fact, faced Hamlet's Elsinore.) That one night he noticed a solar eclipse *"with utter dumb amazement,"* and swore his future over unto astronomy's patience-thinning keeping.

That the uncle resisted, sending the youth to Leipzig University under the care of the tutor Vedel, who was cautioned against such airy nincompoopery. That Tycho obtained a celestial globe "about the size of an orange" he studied surreptitiously, under the bedclothes at night, until the hatchet-visaged Vedel was won over. Then, the years of wandering scholarship: Wittenberg,

Rostock, Basle, Augsburg, ever easy in company noble or low, and ever tearing off excessive chunks of living to quiet his many excessive appetites, and with piffling regard for the consequences.

In Rostock he loses his bridge. They say the argument with Manderup Parsbjerg was simply: which of the two was the better mathematician? Swords were drawn, and Manderup whipped his blade through the bulge of Tycho's nose, as neat as if trimming off a fat-dappled humplet of wurst ("He seems to have taken the loss in good part, and become friends with his adversary"). Any first-year C-minus student of science can tell you about the gold-and-silver-alloy replacement bridge he kept glued snug in its socket, from the fixative in an ointment box he carried.

Whether or not this sanctioned Parsbjerg's claim to superior mathematical prowess, it was Tycho who witnessed the super-nova of 1572 and, recognizing the burst for what it was (and not, as many claimed, a comet), confirmed his hunch with seventeen months of steady observation, then published his theories and tables as *De Nova Stella*. Overnight, nearly, he was a star himself.

On February 11, 1575, King Fredrick 11 of Denmark offered Tycho the use of (really the full despotic control of) the island of Hveen, with granted rights to the rents of all Hveen-dwellers. Uraniborg rose against the blue-brushed steel sky of the Danish Sound, a Camelot–castle–*cum*–16th–century–Disneyland, with running water and statues that spoke via hidden tubes, a library and an alchemical workshop, all facaded by and under a Gothic wedding-cake-of-an-architecture of onion-shaped domes and minarets. There were a printing press and a paper mill driven by water from a chain of fish ponds. Jeppe, the resident dwarf, danced under the banquet tables. Sometimes the pet elk tippled too much beer. The study was decorated lavishly, including a mural of history's eight great astronomers: Ptolemy, Hipparchus, Timocharis, al-Battani, King Alphonso, Copernicus, Tycho

Brahe, and Tycho Brahe's as-yet-unborn son Tychonides.

Yes, and there was a jail for tenants of Hveen who fell behind in the rent. An overbearing landlord, not beyond the greedy squeeze, and pridefully scornful of even his royal patron, Tycho was stripped of his sinecure in 1597, and he moved on with his common-law wife and entourage to Prague, where we find him a favorite of Rudolph II, Archduke of Austria, King of Bohemia-Hungary, and Holy Roman Emperor. We find him at Castle Benatek on the gray edge of morning, florid-faced, huffing, lumbering after a sheet of computations in the fire-light.

His astronomyship *was* computation; for all of his grandiosity and flamboyance, Tycho understood—was really the first of them who understood—that knowing the skies meant, finally, pinpoint and orderly serial records. This, he implemented with a finicky devotion. In a world still awaiting the telescope's invention, Tycho measured the length of a year to within an error of only one second. Before Galileo had ogled a full moon, Tycho had accurately mapped the positions of 777 stars. Arthur Koestler compares his details-keeping to the later arrival of cinema: so continuous are his observations, they come close to forming a moving record.

Tycho had no fiery, hosannah-webworked vision of All of Celestial Wonderment shimmering in his head; but he had the data. He was his age's mainstay archivist of the data. And for some sheets of recent indices, he's running his puffed cheeks blanch then plum, he's roaring in a wobbly circle, he's chasing this hoptoad sneak-a-peek apprentice.

"But my dearest Tycho, these you *gave* to me!" (This could be true.)

"You lie through your rat teeth!" (This could also be true.) "Give here, you cankered sliver of salt pork!"

And now it needs to be said that Tycho is precisely right: in anybody's estimation, Johannes Kepler, genius, is a cankered sliver of salt pork.

~

He was a gnawed bone. He was a hank of a human being, shaped meanly, ulcerated from tongue-root to outlook.

"In me Saturn and the Sun work together in their sextile aspect; therefore my body is small, dry, knobby, my soul suspicious and timid; I reject honors, crouch over books, know no pleasures of life aside from science. All this corresponds to my preference for bitter and sharp tastes, and hard bread."

He was born in 1571, in the small town of Weil in Swabia, "a skinny, sickly, ugly child," Colin Wilson says; and Evan Connell is rhapsodic in expanding on this: "In childhood he endured boils, mange, smallpox, hemorrhoids, constant stomach trouble, and such bad eyesight that he occasionally saw his world doubled or quadrupled." Back to Colin Wilson: "In fact, he was loathed by most of his schoolfellows; he was physically unpleasing (admitting to a 'dog-like horror of baths'), a sneak, a toady, an opportunist and a bookworm."

Angus Armitage says of Kepler: "by turns aggressive, arrogant, servile." Evan Connell: "impatient, sarcastic, cowardly, stingy." His schoolfellows bloodied him frequently. His mother was busy dabbling in witch's matters; Armitage simply calls her "quarrelsome." (Eventually she would be brought to trial for practicing "black arts," a typically mumbling wen-covered old woman.) The father, a mercenary with criminal habits, was rarely at home, and ultimately abandoned the home altogether. The grandparents beat him. A brother was epileptic.

This, then, is a self-portrait by the youth who emerged from what Armitage terms "squalor" and Wilson "purgatory": "I suffered continually from skin ailments, often severe sores, often from the scabs of chronic putrid wounds in my feet which healed badly and kept breaking out again. On the middle finger of my right hand I had a worm, on the left a huge sore. I think I am one of those people whose gall bladder has an opening into the stomach; such people are usually shortlived."

Prickly. Fungal. Feral. A crank. A blighted cabbage. A peptic man. "At Cupinga's I was offered union with a virgin; on New Year's Eve I achieved this with the greatest possible difficulty, experiencing the most acute pains of the bladder..." It seems truly a perversity that, according to Wilson, the youthful Kepler "tried his hand at comedies."

He married stupidly, almost willfully stupidly, a woman thought grossly obese in a time when portliness and beauty were often connected; and Armitage refers to "her descent into melancholy and invalidism." In his novel *Kepler*, John Banville introduces her with the word "grim." Wilson: "mean, stupid, and bad tempered." Easy guile may have been involved in Kepler's decision: she came with a bit of money. Still, it was never enough. They scrimped. She nagged. Nine months from the wedding, the first of Kepler's children arrived, "a boy," Connell puts it, "with seriously deformed genitals." Kepler called this son "a boiled turtle in its shell." There were five children; three of them died.

From this excruciating matrix rose a vision of celestial infrastructure founded on rapture: on July 9, 1595, while chalking a problem onto a slate board, Kepler's cranium suddenly lit inside like a planetarium dome. "Geometry is co-eternal with the mind of God, *is God himself*." And he saw, in a flash of Divine Revelation, "the answer to the design of the solar system": that the orbits of each of the six known planets fit inside the shapes of the "Five Perfect Solids," a tetrahedron, a cube, an octahedron, a dodecahedron, an icosahedron. With that flash, all of Creation had order. Inexplicably, this one great geometrically-foliate rose bloomed from the gorse-patch that was Kepler's earthly existence.

But minor discrepancies, like small relentless djinn, whooshed in when he tried to tie this theory to observation-based calculation. Wilson: "No matter how he juggled the figures, the distances and velocities of the planets refused to fit into his symmetrical moulds. What he needed was more data, more actual observations. And the only man in Europe who could supply those…"

"One last time, you fungus'ed stump: GIVE HERE!" (We may want to read a series of comic book *hic* sounds in between.)

"Nooo, Tyyycho." (This, in the whining of somebody flimsy who's clinging to something so much larger, he knows he could be flicked off like a shoofly from a plough-ox's rump.)

~

Richard Grossinger: "Kepler sought only the freedom to work on his problem and to have unhindered access to the records. When Tycho hired Kepler, it was to complete his own system. He was the nobleman, Kepler the commoner. Deep down he might have understood that Kepler had the better mind, but he lived in a courtly world, centuries from such an admission. Their collaboration was interrupted on numerous occasions by…" I SHALL BITE YOUR SWALES OF LARD INTO A BOLT OF LACE, IF YOU SO MUCH AS NEAR ME! "…temper outbursts."

Still, their starry projects inched ahead.

I don't even know who wins this round of their two-year tug-of-war. I know it's starting to snow: the parapets glitter like mica. I know a maid will find them hours later, curled up on the hearth floor, drunken slop-breath creakily bellowsing in and out. Two grooms will heft them to their separate chambers (groaning under Tycho's more generous poundage). Kepler, back to his severe wife in the room described by Banville as "a cramped brown box." The Master, back to the rises and folds of Christine, in their gilt four-poster Überastronomer's bed.

It must be, one of them does have that list of calculations crumpled away in his sash—who knows? The grime of nearly four hundred years intervenes. The specifics are foxed in the corners, dust-clumped, eaten by acid content.

What I see clearly enough from this far is a living diorama of Philolaus's cosmic paradigm: a "Central Fire," and these two bodies in orbit around it, invisible to each other.

"Give here, you parasite-slug from a milk-herring's bum!"

"Stand off, I warn you, Oh Most Splendiferous Comet-Addled Hogshead-for-Brains!"

Tycho and Kepler, Earth and Counter-Earth, Gimme and No-Way, around and around until they churn down into butter.

3.

This was in Prague, where the streets are twisted. Maybe in some of the people's hearts, the veins were twisted, too. Such ugly things they did! Still, there were good peoples also—*kind* peoples. Boys and girls got married, you make faces but they were happy to go to *Purim* dances together, to open *Chanukah* presents. But always, twisted streets, and twisted buildings, and long long shadows where the evil things could happen and nobody see! One night...

And once again, with that same stale bait of hers, Lucille Maxine Mandelbaum reeled us in.

～

Rudolph II made his court the Hradcany, the royal castle at Prague, and this decision brought unexpected prosperity to the city. Foreign merchants—from Saxony, Nuremburg, Italy—settled in colonies inside the city-walls, supplying the needs of a spangled flux of Rudolph's nobles. Powerful Jewish families, often bankers, established themselves in a compound; one of these, the Meyzl, was even given permission to build its own palace. Banners, ballrooms, irony: all of the hallmarks of cosmopolitan living were erected in the midst of the native Czech proletariat day-to-day squabble and drone.

The Hradcany, fortress-walled and built on a hill, provided ample security for the court. Its groups of royal and seigniorial dwellings, churches, and gardens, formed a small town in themselves; and here the otherworldly Holy Roman Emperor Rudolph, bearer of the crown of Charlemagne, devoted his days to his misty pursuits.

His private menagerie swelled with fauna exotica: cockatoos, a dour torpid camel, albino apes, a deer with antlers clasped like praying hands, an anteater, silver foxes zebra-striped in melanomas. Alchemical laboratories were located in a lane along the walls; and here, exquisite transformations in their alembics blazed all night. Select visitors might be led past life-size wax-work figures from the Old Testament (or similar figures in pornographic poses, either with their waxy selves or in a scripted orgy-of-sorts with human participants), displays of ore and drift-wood in fantastical shapes, collections of coins or ancient painted bones or petrified animal droppings, clockwork dummies that lifted mugs of ale (and one, its skirts), a group of jester hermaphrodites, steam-driven toys, or Albrecht Dürer's *Festival of the Rose Garlands,* which supposedly was carried all the way from Venice by hand. Or one might see the marble plaque commemorating "the Pole Sendivogius"—he transmutated a particum of base metal to gold for the Emperor, and was praised in verse by Mordecai of Delle, the court's alchemical poet.

In a castle of wonders Rudolph bewondered himself away from the world—as others would use the term "sequestered." This is what the textbooks say repeatedly: "eccentric." He neglected affairs of state, consorted with grooms…the charges are adamant, and credible enough. But one might just as easily say he was a scholar, and "enlightened" in the best sociopolitical sense. A nascent feeling of equal commingling occurred in the new Prague, and the checker-tiled dining halls received the likes of the famous mage John Dee, of course Brahe and Kepler, the presumed occultist the Rabbi Loew. One tends to see it in terms of the court of King Arthur, or the Left Bank of Stein.

But these were not good times—if any are—for the less-than-select: lip-pickers, orphans, droughted farmers, women of almost any station, religious minorities. Remember, for instance, that Kepler's mother was only one of tens of thousands accused of plying witchcraft, in the mania that filled the air of Europe with burning human flesh. Inquisitors used saw-bladed forceps. Husbands pointed out wives; and daughters, their mothers. Hair in a birthmark, and you were suspected. To drive long pins into the breasts or vaginal lips of suspected witches was a pious fulfillment. Voices whispered out of the air, invisible tongues licked bodies in sleep. Crops failed, people took ill overnight, and somebody—always *somebody*—was responsible, somebody sleepwalked, somebody scowled The Devil's Look, somebody worshipped under the wrong roof.

"Witch's gatherings were *Sabbats* or, to the anti-Semitic, *Synagogues*…" When you ran out of witches, you always had Jews. Where the streets met the river, they twisted.

⁓

This is what they would do, a man named Brother Thaddeus— how do you say? *incited* his people to do this. He would yell to them, the Jews they use the blood of Christian babies in their ceremonies. (Here she'd mouth a separate large sphere for each word): They. Drink. The. Blood. And then one of his no-goods, they would find a dead baby, and put it a secret when no one was looking inside the house of a Jew, and *pf!* they had proof.

Nobody was safe. A Jew could go to market, buy a basket of onions, and on the way home, *pf!* (and once again): A. Pitchfork. In. The. Throat!

So what they needed, like these bangbang guys from your comic book things, to look out for them—how would you say?

"A vigilante!"

Yes, yes, so. A wigilante.

~

They had fasted for seven days and nights, and had not lain with their wives.

Now, on the second day of the month of Adar of the year Jewish Calendar 5340, after midnight, neither with stealth nor obviously, the three men had attended the ritual bath—the *Mikveh*—and then to Rabbi Loew's house, where they chanted the *Hazoth* and Psalms, and the Rabbi read several chapters of the *Sefer Yezirah* aloud. The other two let the familiar rituals wash, like the bath water, over them. This was the part they knew, and so were safe in. Then the Rabbi had snuffed the candles; they heard him leave the room, presumably to give a goodbye stroke to Pereleh's forehead as she slept. He returned, and he carried three torches.

Isaac was dragging his leg, result of an accident with a brick merchant's sledge. The Rabbi Loew looked tenderly at his son-in-law, at the asymmetrical track he left. A few steps behind them came the labored, half-asthmatic breath of the Rabbi's pupil, Jacob ben Chayim Sasson. It sounded like some mired animal forcing its way up a muck slope. And so these are the three the Lord chooses, Loew thought, for protecting His troubled people. Loew was sixty-seven years—vigorous, yes, but sixty-seven. He shook his head.

At last they reached the outskirts. In the distance, on the other side of the Moldau, velvet pasturelands receded to the horizon. If it were day, he knew, they'd look like unrolled bolts of deep jade-green and russet: wind would give them nap.

But it was black out, these three were cloaked in black, and even their fitful torch-light they made sure was blocked on the city side by a hasty lean-to of garbage boards and branches.

And chanting the Psalms, on their knees, from the cool and grayish insides of a clay-bed there, they fashioned the shape of a man—"three ells in length," as one source puts it, "and with all members."

"The Golem lay before them with its face turned toward heaven. It lay there as if dead."

The Rabbi Loew bade his son-in-law Isaac ben Simson walk seven times around the body, right to left, reciting certain *Zirufim* charms—for Isaac embodied Fire.

When this was done, the clay body grew red, like fire.

Then the Rabbi Loew bade Jacob ben Chayim Sasson walk seven times around the body, left to right, reciting the formula for his element—it was Water.

And when this was done, the fire-red was extinguished, and life's immemorial moistures laved their appropriate places, and hair scraggled over the head, and nails shielded fingers and toes.

Then Rabbi Loew walked once around the body, and in its lax mouth placed a slip of parchment inscribed with the *Schem*, the name of God; and all three bowed to the four directions, and Rabbi Loew recited *And He breathed into his nostrils the breath of life, and man became a living soul*—for Rabbi Loew was Air.

And as Fire, Water, and Air stood about it—frightened, hopeful, filthied, they were, and their atoms dancing crazily in place—Earth rose. Earth opened its eyes, and saw these three with their own mouths lax for a moment, gawk-faced, pulled like human putty between solemnity and whooping.

The Golem was mute. He was a blank slate. But was perfectly formed, and potent.

And they dressed him in the garments of a synagogue sexton. The Rabbi said, "Thy name is Joseph. We have given thee form, from the clay men walk on. Thou shalt lodge in my home; and sit at my table; and make God's people, and mine, thy people. It will be thy task to protect the Jews from persecution. Thou must obey my commands, and look to the ranks of the enemy, and be as a wall betwixt. Do you, Joseph, understand?"

The Golem nodded assent. And from a lean-to branch they made him a torch, so he would look as one who had accompanied them from the city.

"So."

And four men walked back into Prague.

⌒

You see? He was to be the Rabbi's eyes and ears. To go around, look, hear, these plots from no-good peoples were making. A spy!

⌒

We saw. A spy—invisible, invincible.

Was *this* how Lucille discovered the Discount Paint Prince's infidelity? Could she sit in her faded-burgundy brocade chair, and all the while have some access to a mystical infiltrator in her employ? I think the answer is yes, though it may be a needlessly rococo way of saying *intuition*.

"Man, she knows EVERYTHING! I bet you she can smell her cheap cologne on him, when he's sleeping!"

We knew everything, too: seen movies, heard jokes. We knew The Other Woman always trails a pennant of "cheap cologne," she applies it in buckets, she sphritzes it from sea-blue gem-like atomizers on body parts we'd never seen and could only crudely imagine.

"Noschel, he smells like an opened can of paint, that's all."

"I tell you, she sees EVERYTHING!"

"Then you'd better stop jerking off, jerkoff."

Eloquence. Giggles. We were kings of that small room, and Kong was stunned by our repartee into a state approaching the comatose.

I'd dawdle back to my own home then, and I don't know what Noschel did beneath the covers while waiting for sleep, but *I* jerked off—the bimbo would come to me, slinky, succubus-like, I'd hear her gasp at my wordmastery, oh Itzie was as nothing compared to my fourteen-year-old's magnetism! She'd purr, she'd curl up, she'd open.

And so (even before those early sexual urges—say, as early as six) I felt a kind of empathy for Itzie. I saw, though I couldn't have put it in words: how he transplanted himself from Europe, starting with nothing here but a satchel of greenhorn moxie; how he sweated a business into existence, okay it wasn't a dynasty, but a thriving concern he earned past-the-max with every groaned-out overtime shipment of siding tipped onto Chicago ice, and the winch crew, and the insurance; how he only wanted, like anyone else, the vitalmost rush up his humdrum nerves for the sadly little while we call a life; how he only wanted belonging, here in the popsong backslap that's a salesman's America; how he was "with it," he affected a taste for glitzier versions of jazz, he knew when a deal was "copasetic," and here was his wife with her *blintzes*–accent held stubbornly to like a talisman.

And Lucille would never do anything slinky, I knew that, I knew that he loved her, he did, but I saw her give the delicate heart-shaped dram of *Midnight Rendezvous* the stare of a fishwife considering a silver slipper hooked up out of the ocean waters: *pfui!*

Maybe she was the one who, even before the bright peroxide sun burst over Itzie's horizon, turned her back on their own glitch-bridging intimacies. She carped, I knew that: at Noschel, at Itzie, she yanked away at me as if for practice, or mistrusting my own mother's diligence. I couldn't have said, those years of nights I tossed in bed like a salad of ethics, if Itzie's longterm dalliance was a weakness in him or a strength. Those two polarities mottled him, shadow and light, in my imagination.

But when I would think of Lucille, she was in shadow completely, rigid in her brocade chair alone at night, cast out of his most vibrant caring, and vigilant—pathetically so—for signs of that abandonment: a creak on the stair as he snuck in, maybe (sure, why not) a sniff of sweat and cheap cologne from his throat.

No matter how you cut it, she was the victim; yes, and in the chemistry of empathy, more flowed from me in her direction than his. I had a child's tiny idea of what small daily durability it took for her to face her mirror, smooth the folds out of her pride, and simply walk to the corner supermarket as if her entire world weren't nudged off-orbit. I see her sitting in shadow, telling us tales of awe and terror lurking in Old World shadows, and herself attuned to clues from the shadow-life Itzie was leading: something of her (strength, I guess I'd have to call it) gleams its way through all of that.

On some nights I'd have empathy left over for the bimbo—what was *her* life like, when Itzie was bantering baseball stats with Noschel and me, and Cap looked up from a book with pure rambunctiousness in his eyes, and…then I'd lose the image, it frizzled away at its edges, but I knew I'd seen the start of an evening of emptiness for both of them, and I shivered to have been spared it.

I was six, or ten, or fourteen: how much empathy was a person *supposed* to feel; how many other lives did I need to take on, in the slide toward sleep; how great a weight of them could I bear (as if *my* life weren't burden aplenty) and when would I be old enough to shuck it; when could I walk the Magic Walk in reverse around these figures and lay them back down on the banks of the Moldau, (now I was drowsy), back in the Earth…

~

Quoting Lyall Watson: "DNA is a rather fragile molecule on its own, very easily broken by mechanical stresses, even those as simple as stirring it in solution. It is also easily damaged by ultra-violet radiation, which is certainly very powerful in space and must have been prevalent on the earth before enough ozone was formed to produce our atmosphere. Therefore DNA if it existed at all, was a most unlikely first choice for genetic material."

He's looking for the origin of the origin of life: *the* first and utterly singular proto-unit of anything. It needed to be self-forming; it needed to acquire and hold information; it needed the ability to replicate this information exactly (as DNA does) and yet have the capability (as DNA does) to evolve. And he says, "Crystals are vivid examples of the capacity of matter to organize itself. They are regular geometric forms which seem to arise spontaneously and then to replicate themselves in a steady manner.

"The evolution of life may have begun with the existence of a suitable crystal, probably a very small one, relatively insoluble in water. A colloidal material would be ideal, and none is in fact more common, or better suited to the needs of a primitive gene, than clay."

He postulates "organic molecules drifting down out of interstellar space to infect, vitalize, and be organized by the crystal clays of earth." Clays can even natively "build up patterns of organic molecules between their silicate layers," and these would be incorporated into the next automatic crystalline replication, and then the next: "You have in a bed of clay everything necessary for the acquisition and inheritance of new characteristics. As more and more of the information in the silicates was transformed to the organic molecules, the clay would cease to control and take on a more passive role as a protective clamp. Cell walls could indeed evolve…"

Quoting Nathan Ausubel: "In its literal meaning the word *golem* means lifeless, shapeless matter—into which the one who has discovered the *Schem,* God's Ineffable Name, can by its mystic means breathe the impulse of life."

$\sim$

So he sat down in a corner to wait for his—how do you say, what they tell him to do, like orders.

"His instructions?"

Okay, to wait for his instruckations.

4.

All day, a dither had rippled through Castle Benatek, felt by the least of the grooms and chambermaids, and emanating splashily, continuously, from the two astronomical impresarios—who, by dusk and the guest's arrival, had managed to control their grumping enough for it to resemble two chained mastiffs which (while wild for each other's jugular) halted, by virtue of these restraints, a good clear two or three feet from actually sinking teeth in windpipe.

Tycho was in the scullery peeking, through wreaths of greasy air, into the kitchen. He was agitated, uneasiness burbled inside him. This guest, the Emperor himself had recommended him as a mage; who could tell, but the secrets of ancient alchemy or even the lore of Cabala might be talked about around the table, divinated secrets might have conversational light shed over their surfaces! And yet Tycho was The Great Man of His Age, it should seem as if *he* were the one being courted. Even to himself, he didn't care to admit anticipation. And then, of course, this fellow was...well, even with Rudolph's encomium, still...but it could go unmentioned under the circumstances.

"Basting be damned! This is time for the sauce of crushed snails!" The kitchen women swiveled like a troupe of dancers to face his voice. They were clumped at a boar, a whole one, spitted, its eyes long gouged from their sockets and fed to a favorite hound. "You score the flesh just slightly, then you rub in the sauce, with heads of garlic..." He stopped in mid-intrusion. They were dumbfounded, seeing him here. He never was here. He saw now, this was a tactical blunder, plainly betraying his anxiousness.

"Do as you will. Have deer or use the sturgeons instead if you will," and he attempted to leave a casual flutter behind him in the doorway, although the hand that made it looked more like one of the smoked hams from over the chopping block.

Upstairs in a nook he'd turned into a one-shelf personal library, Kepler was grousing. Last week, both of them had decided tonight's conversation would be in private—the names by which demons are summoned, the movements of planets by guiding spirit-bodies, these are not fit subjects for serving-girls' ears. So it would be the three of them only. And as the day wore on, and he and Tycho talked of sundry mundane matters, it came to be clear—though never directly, but by an insubstantially gassy intimation—that it was expected he, Johannes Kepler, seeker of the shape of God's Creation, should pour the wine and offer the foods and remove the used platters, he, Kepler!

It stung as if a doctorphysick had stitched a nettle into his brain. For knowledge's sake, he told himself, he would do this. For learning. For one more key, perhaps, to the chest where the constellations were heaped for the taking like gold coins. He lay fetally squinched on the floor of his alcove, saying it repeatedly, *for knowledge*, as if the words were an unction that might soak helpfully into this hurt.

And so it was, when a great red yolk of a sun oozed out of itself, into the char haze on the horizon, that one of Benatek's carriages shuffled to the gate and the Rabbi Yehudah Loew was escorted into the main hall.

～

It was all a matter of noses.

Castle Benatek was twenty miles north of Prague, and so there was much of "how-was-the-trip" as a means of easing the chatter's initial rigidity, of sizing one another up. The Rabbi politely declined a goblet of wine, so lost a prop with which to emphasize or conceal, although he often made a small tent of his hands in front of his face, as if it helped translate pure thought into the language of social visit.

Tycho used his goblet as a decorating of his expansive gesturing—an arm would swoop the air, and the flambeaux-light would gleam along the crystal swell or up the spiraled stem. In front of his own face, Kepler kept his goblet protectively scrunched, as if it contained some kind of prophylactic nostrum against the Plague. He awkwardly kept it held between himself and Tycho, firmly, even when replenishing the other's wine from a leather-cased decanter.

One notices these minutiae of interchemistry. So Tycho's, the Rabbi realized, was a lush, voluptuary's nose; it understood society, satiety, and no doubt satyriety, if not now then at times in the past; its metal saddle (though some attempt had been made to paint it a flesh color) startled even when one was prepared for it, and seemed to be the stamp of authenticity to those tales of extravagance.

"...a catalogue the like of which is unknown!" and a dive-and-soar of the goblet accentuated his point. He was talking about his exemplary list of the stars, there was a charmingly childlike pride in this, as if his charts actually granted him proprietary rights in the heavens. "Later, I will show you." The empty goblet made a subtle flounce in Kepler's direction, to be refilled.

And the nose of the other? A sniffler's nose. A sniveler's nose. And two or three times, as if shielded by the goblet, he picked it— once, giving such a hypochondriac concentration to the color or consistency on his fingertip, you'd swear he was trying to augur the future by reading this smear. But the Rabbi knew a radish, though gnarled and bitter, has a wonderful sharpness to it. This Kepler... The radish can burn. *Hoy!* hadn't Pereleh's horseradish made him weep? Well this Kepler was burning in-side, was sharp. Whatever his vision was of the grand celestial vault, it was as large as the vault itself, and as breath-taking.

All this the Rabbi saw, while they tried undoing the tent of his hands, unweaving his fifty-four years of beard, uncoupling one word from another for study.

～

"Ah, lovely, thank you, thank you. But no, you understand...the dietary restrictions..."

He was staring nearly face-to-face at a monstrous boar, its eyesockets crammed with hardboiled eggs on which an anatomist-chef had painted green irises; some kind of sauce, with floating bits of unguessable detritus, was hardening over its back and sides. To the left, on a separate platter, the haunch and leg of a deer poked up at the ceiling, its hoof still crowning it—in fact, the hoof had been gilded and covered with paste-gems, to point out the metaphor. Right, on a white cloth, three whole sturgeon were piled; each was thickly sheathed in a gleaming casing of whole-grain pepper, and the final effect was of three ornately-pommeled swords in their scabbards.

Loew felt honored, sickened, uncomfortable with refusal but smugly righteous in naysaying—altogether overwhelmed by his own multipartite response.

"Ah, yes, of course, the restrictions…Rabbi, we apologize, myself and my colleague. Ah, some substitution perhaps…" How stupid they'd been! How stupid, this Jew and his finicky eating! Stupid, stupid, stupid!

"I thank you, this is generous. But, no, please, understand. The restrictions are very encompassing. Anyway," the tent opened into a stylized shrug, "I have recently been fasting…seven days… a minor religious matter. It would not do, for an old man's system, to feast this richly this soon." He thought he could hazard a witticism by now. "*You* feast, we'll talk, perhaps I'll have occasion to eat my words."

Tycho chuckled politely; it was lost on Kepler. By this time, massive amounts of the meal were disappearing into Tycho's face although, from long experience eating with priests and governors, he magically made it look dainty. Kepler picked at his food with less relish than at his nose. He ate almost nothing and that, reluctantly—then how did he give an intense impression of slovenliness and waste? He had a kind of anti-magic that made everything repellently mundane.

Now he spoke: "The dietary restrictions, yes. They must"—he searched about cunningly for a compliment—"they must increase the pleasure in what you *can* eat." He smiled greasily, pleased the social obligation was out of the way now. "But your people, Rabbi...we hear their restrictions do not extend to the study of astrological matters." He tried to make it half a question.

Stupid, stupid! Tycho groaned softly around a bite of boar's brains. Couldn't this Swabian upstart manage one politic word! Did his questioning need to be put with the subtlety of a plank's-slap to a hog's ass? Even so, Tycho found himself tense in awaiting the answer.

"There is a saying we have: *Let the people attend to their Sabbath candles; the Lord will attend to the stars.*"

So that's how it went: thrust, parry.

Over Tycho's dessert—"But Rabbi, tell us: it must be such an exalting thing, to come prepared to a learning of Cabala..."

"I will tell you, when I was little, a boy, in Worms-on-the-Rhine, my Uncle was given, in payment once, a bull. This animal!—you could stare into its eyes ten miles deep. It was very mysterious. And it was a bull, it had a wild will of its own! It ran away,oh perhaps twice a week it did this. We'd search the hills—but no bull. We'd call its name. My Uncle once drove a cow in heat through the hill land—no; no bull. When it was ready, from wherever it went off to, it returned. But we needed to wait. *It* came to *us*. There was no beseeching it."

∼

What—did they think he devoted night and day to swirling sedimental gunk around the bellies of alchemical vessels!

For God, for the Word and the Will of the Lord, he, the Rabbi Yehuda Loew, *was* a vessel!

～

And then, with that thought having burned off the difficult conversational buildup, his spirit felt lighter. Maybe the late hour, too. Vessels... He looked at a porcelain tankard sitting on the table not far down, the Bavarian kind shaped into the wide-faced caricature of some human type.

The great Tycho was holding forth on his own revisionist tinkering with the Copernican system. Loew puffed out his cheeks with globes of air, and tried to lower his head as far down into his shoulders as possible, then he held the position. He looked like a turtle fashioned out of fresh dough. Tycho glanced at Kepler, Kepler back to Tycho. They both turned back to Loew with flabbergastion overcoming them.

"The Emperor Rudolph—*sssh*."

And suddenly all three were laughing, genuine laughter (Kepler's more a cackle, but no less genuine.) Maybe the late hour. Maybe their skittishly forming sense of common purpose: flinging one's self, a candle in hand, at the endlessly dark Unknown.

～

They were staring a trillion miles into it now. (Of course they didn't know this—guessed it maybe, feared it certainly, held on to an idea of "hundred," "thousands" at the most, as if infinity could be grabbed by its vasty lapels and dragged closer.)

"Look; see?"

They were on one of the especially-constructed balconies. By turns they were sighting along an arm of the *Instrumentum Parallacticum* Tycho had created for tallying heaven.

"I see two stars—are there two stars?"

"My friend, I just myself saw two Johannes Keplers make

∴ 64 ∴

water over two balcony rails."

Rabbi Loew, a while before, had rumpled about inside the voluminous folds of his somber attire, bringing forth an ingeniously hinged (a couple of decades later, one would say "telescoping") metal wine cup. "Your goblets...please do not be offended, they cannot touch my lips. But now, I think, a spot of your good wine in my own cup, yes?"

So they're weaving around up here, and squinting, aiming, trying to bring those distant flaming asterisks as up-close as the staring hardboiled eyes of the boar.

"It doesn't matter, I think. We could double the number or halve the number and still—look, look—the miracle of it all remains stable, it plucks the string from your balls to the skin of your brain."

"Perhaps. But I think I shall count them anyway. The Flood was forty years, Methuselah lived nine hundred thirty-seven years: even miracles come in numbers."

The banker of stars. And his colleague their architect, building now his little pee arch while he yodels up at that band of sheer grandeur.

And now a hound in the yard picks it up, and gives out with its own doggy yodel. And then another hound, and another, and three men singing an old folk ditty together, "The Jolly Voyagers," three exotic feathers jauntily cocked from the hat Castle Benatek makes in silhouette on the moonflooded country.

～

But they couldn't convince him to stay the night. "We have a saying: *The sun will rise without your assistance*. And another: *But it never hurts to help*. I have prayers to lead in the morning, I must."

"Then I will rouse those loutish carriage boys who brought you here, and warn them at least to avoid the stinking streets of the tannery district on your way back."

"No, no, that route is the most direct. I am a Jew, and have been a Jew for sixty-seven years, and I am accustomed to making my way to my prayers through the stenches this world offers."

At the main door, Kepler tugged once at Loew's sleeve. He couldn't leave it alone: "Have you any last…call it wisdom…"

"Wisdom? No, no, I don't pretend to…" It trailed off. And then he said, an afterthought, "Together you make one person, you know. Two…aspects. Use him well, my friends."

～

And Tycho thought: "*That* niggling slitherer?"

And Kepler thought: "*That* bellysloshing bombastinating professor of orotundity?"

And they both thought: "Funny old Jew."

And Loew thought: "If the stars *could* come as near as people do, would they also seem so different, one from the other?…" and then he floated off, out of the carriage, into the country of jostle and drowse.

～

Tycho didn't know, or Kepler, or Frau Kepler, what the entire staff of Castle Benatek down to the dog-boy knew in the pit of its ragtag collection of souls—the lady Christine, she surely ruled this isolated world, ruled master Tycho himself by the tides of her big-boned comfortable body and by the whispered innuendoed advice she'd offer after their sheets were love-soaked through, ruled the moods of the man and so the sub-moods of the coterie who catered to the man, knew every pleat in a hanging and every tinny hour-sound of every zodiac-decorated clock, knew what the gruel-faced Kepler slattern said to the ferret-faced Kepler wretch at their most intimate chamberpot play, and if she didn't know statistics on the phases of the moon, she knew how all of this community moved as a consequence of her own cycles.

What she knew now was that Tycho should be senselessly beached beside her, from his spate of social tra-la-la—should be snoring that wine imbibed with the Jew and the Kepler-man out of his system. After all, tomorrow day he needed poring over those damnable astronomical tables, making of his awareness a forceps for moving ant's-egg decimal points from place to place; and then tomorrow night, one more over-garrulous needlessly sumptuous dinner somewhere in the city… Baron Rosenberg's, she recalled. Yes, normally now he'd be a buttocky bulk in the coverlets at her side, all wine-unconscious with a small sour flume of wine breath. So: where *was* he?

I'll tell you. Up in his "thinking room," where he kept the lapis-and-cherrywood working model of "his" solar system. Yes—but he wasn't looking at that, he was looking…where was he looking?

What the Jew had said. Two "aspects." He'd been born a twin. He'd dragged that dead brother, that inside-out of himself, around now for fifty-four years. Conferred with him in dream, contended with him in nightmare, turned to see a flash of him, a fog of him, some fabulous indication (never more than that) of an elseness sharing his name.

And now this Kepler had come. What the Jew said. Tycho drunk, but not so dullard-drunk he couldn't recount the entire fated chain of events that finally bound the two of them together.

As early as 1596, when Tycho received a copy of Kepler's *Mysterium Cosmographicum,* he had invited the younger man to visit him. But Tycho was in Denmark; Kepler, Austria. The six hundred miles between forbade it.

"Then, in the summer of 1598—by which time Tycho was already on his way across Europe—fate took a hand," is how Colin

Wilson says it. Austria's Roman Catholicism shaped, at long last, an official stand against Protestantism, including an order for Protestant teachers to leave the country "on pain of death." Kepler, who had already been fined for burying his daughter (dead of meningitis) with Protestant rites, recognized time to move on. "And once more fate intervened; a councillor of the Emperor Rudolph happened to be in Graz, and offered to take Kepler in his suite back to Prague—where Tycho had just been appointed Imperial Mathematicus." January 1, 1600—the first day of the new century—Johannes and Barbara Kepler set out.

The stars of birth pull strings that dance a person down the staircase of his destiny—or do they? It was late, he was mushy, and Tycho half gave-in to slumber there at the insufficient, spindle-leg note-taking desk. It seemed sometimes the continent itself had shrugged and upbuckled to roll the two of them into this castle together, like pieces of a tabletop game.

If a ghost returns to the scene of its death, did Tycho's twin return to Tycho? Doesn't every person have a person who's his balance, isn't God's intention symmetry? Why...

When Christine opened the door, a candle in hand, and his shadow leaped out of him onto the wall, he shrieked. He goggled at it in amazement.

She patiently led him back down to bed; his breeches were drenched in wine pee.

5.

Cap smuggled drugs into the country, through his stable of beautiful fashionmodel-type operatives. Cap built atomic robots for the government. Cap was a motorcycling version of a medieval troubadour, wandering kingdom to kingdom, trading nights' lodgings for poems. Cap this. Cap that. Cap Wonder Guy disguised as an everyday office boy but wielding mystic lightningbolts of power, like electrified javelins.

All into our freshman year at college, Noschel extrapolated Caps with the fierce dedication of a cosmologist trying to figure out expanding or contracting. Cap the race car driver. Cap the Interpol spy.

That year I did meet Cap. She was beautiful, like her mother: I saw the deep reserve and intermittent passion that knocked the youthful Itzie for a loop. And I would call her that occasionally, a nickname: "Cap," I'd say, once I'd explained it to her, and she'd give out the kind of unashamedly girlish laughter I'd only known grown women to give on the movie screen, then maybe tease a nipple-tip across my lower lip.

We'd met in a community poetry workshop I'd been driven to by the tongs-and-chainsaw ruthlessness of my college workshop. Cap (well, really Stephanie, but I called, so I'm calling, her Cap) had never set foot on a college campus, though she had managed in eighteen years to boogie her way through much of this world. She *smelled* of the world to me, of a dangerous, beckoning world I hadn't known but ached for.

She knew all the angles, she'd conned her Scheherazade way out of countless corners, she'd slept curved in some of the tighter spots with a various list of cohorts. Sometimes after making love I'd nuzzle her side and a musk came out of her armpits that wavily spoke to me of nights in smoky cellar jazz clubs. She knew things about human nature, and the body it coursed through, so far ahead of me, she was like an advance scout sent out years before—though in fact I was just a touch older. This guy, that guy, the commune in Frisco…all by herself she outnumbered me.

She was, as my mother might say, "a free spirit." One week she wouldn't shave her legs: "I like the hair, it's the real animal me, I don't need to deform my natural self for any men." The next, she'd greet me at the door of her apartment wearing nothing but a fuschia-lamé garter-belt and filmy hose, her legs as smooth as the dreams of porcelain figurines.

She was insatiable. Sex over, and then more sex over, she'd wake and ride my leg, she'd wet it lavishly and then slide back and forth on that rich slick from her own insides, until her purring nurtured me back into action. Remember: I'd never been with a woman before. I would have thought it impossibly exotic to fumble mechanically in a backseat with some half-begrudging English major, stiff-shouldered, and wondering what the big effing deal was. In a way, Cap ruined me: no one would be this exciting again for years. I know that too, I wasn't stupid about her enormous poise and vitality.

What she saw in me? After all, she'd had men—real *men*. But I think that was it: she relaxed in me, she *practiced* in me, as one might leisurely try out new maneuvers in an ocean liner's pool, who was used to swimming at risk through the ocean. And she wanted to be an artist, she said; there were tentative faery-world watercolors, with sky-blue and blushed-rouge backgrounds, scattered about. Of course I encouraged her. She needed to believe me, so did.

At first, I thought it might be Noschel—that once we had made the connection, knew who we were in the scheme of Itzie's bifurcated life, she saw in me a bridge to coming to know more of his legal child, her half-brother, maybe coming to know that other, domestically-boundaried existence her absentee father led amid the chenille and chopped liver-scent of Lucille's domain. I assumed she'd eagerly rise to meet the level of Noschel's obsessions.

I was wrong, of course. She was grained with the smudge of experience, and hadn't spent her adolescence fantasizing. She enjoyed Itzie's company, the few times a season she'd see him.

He "was good to" her mother. That's all she needed. Noschel was just science-fiction to her, and it couldn't compare to the details of her own diary.

And with her, in her, I was also billions of miles distant from those childhood concerns. One day I was pal-ing around with Noschel ("Do you wanna go to the movies tonight?" "Well, yeah, but I've got this neighborhood poetry workshop starting." "Oh—*that*."); the next, I was stroking her mound, her *actual mound*, with my *actual hand*, a mole's coat of a mound, and all of planet Earth, Noschel included, fell away to the size of a cat's-eye marble while we floated huge and fumey through the universe.

That's how we learned it, that night. "Do you like it?" (So coyly.) "*Oh* do I like it! A sweet little beast, even better to pet than Kong." "KONG?"

You can imagine the rest.

~

But planet Earth, it turns out, has long ties and cunning grapnels.

And the body has *many* lessons to teach. My mother was dying. Nobody used that word, the doctors especially—one was fond of "looking forward to a turnaround"—but the Story of Dying Slowly has its own vocabulary, and once you learn it you can't be fooled. She'd rumble up phlegm, the color of army camouflage—that bird-boned woman, friend of Lucille's, my mother, a snip a stiff breeze could fly off with. On bad days she hadn't the strength to bring it up, and then it hardened to a crust inside her chest.

I was already leading two lives, half between Cap's thighs, and half between one class and another in Noschel's insistent company: two worlds (two *me's*, I suppose) I refused to let meet. And now this third enormity. Something had to go, and Noschel went. I still sat beside him in classes. By rote, and rite, we still covered the same gabbed ground. But I wasn't interested any longer in calling Marsha Glickman's breasts torpedoes. "You're half-dead," he'd say and be right, I was—to him. I felt traitorous, really, abandoning him to childhood while I took my first dreadful steps out of it.

And meanwhile, she was abandoning me—my mother. Half-dead and drifting over the line. Or did you think I meant Cap? Because a few months later she left. I'd shown her the college campus. It would be a treat for her, and a special pocket of expertise I had that she didn't (those seemed strikingly few). In the cafeteria corner Arnie Fleischer was blowing air out of his eye, he was fluffing a thumb-width of notebook paper across the table. She wanted him. Or maybe she just didn't want me any longer. It was easy enough—in a week he was a regular in her bed. He quit school. I heard he went back to Frisco with her, for a while: construction work, LSD.

And at the end it seemed easy enough for my mother. For someone so bent on rejoining the earth, she looked strangely ready to spiral away on a thermal of hospital corridor air: a papery husk, a used-up Chinese lantern of a person. Although for someone so airy, she clearly was heading soilward, gravitybound, into the fingerbone clutches six cliché feet below.

I think she was reconciled to both of those only possible selves. We'd talk, between the indifferent ministrations of nurses. Endless rosary-lengths of small bright coated pills. The needles. Tests she'd return from, with a few more slices shaved off. We'd talk, in a way more intimate than we'd been since I first set my needful mouth to her breast in a different wing of that same building, foggily long ago.

I didn't remember my father. Hers was my first experienced death. And then visiting hours were over, I'd drive through

Chicago's frightening mess of traffic to my first experienced ecstasy of the flesh. The pull was far too strong, it wouldn't let me sink into my grief—Cap naked, wrapped in a fake fur bear rug; Cap suggesting we play she's my nurse. I'd make her nipples swell and rise like a choir-of-two implored upon to stand up and fill the room with orisons.

In her own understanding of how things work, she must have thought she was comforting me. She was, too; but the loves I felt in such opposite directions; the two most different sweats I churned out; the immensely adversarial and yet horribly overlaid views of the unclothed female body those months provided... I'd stare at the ceiling for hours, confused, with the question that kept me tormenting myself when I was six, or ten, or fourteen: how many other lives did I need to take on, in the slide toward sleep?

The end was thankfully gentle. One lunchtime she didn't awake. The nurse was left foolishly holding her hypodermic in the air, like a clock's second hand with no time to point to.

That night I didn't see Cap, or the next, or the next. When I did again, she was delicate and sweet: she understood that's what I needed, more than the pretzelwork of our legs. A week later, thinking some new factor would liven our chemistry, I suggested she visit my campus. There was Arnie Fleischer, faithfully honing his freakish ocular skill.

She was back with my father now, whatever that meant and wherever it was. "We'll be one again soon," she'd told me. I remember they left me alone with her, an unusually sensitive gesture, for a moment in the hospital room. A smell laced the air not unlike the rank sea tang I'd come to recognize as Cap's flushed body at orgasm.

∼

"But everyone at *Rosie-O's* will be dressed up…I know! My mom lives near here, and I have some extra clothes in her closet. Let's go."

So it was that simple. I met the bimbo—Tabitha—at last. "But everybody calls me Tabby," she said, "Itz calls me Tabby." Who? Oh—he was "Itz" here. Here, where they chatted the latest chichi buzzword into the night, he was Itz or, ritzily, Isadore.

"Steph, honey, your clothes are folded into the armoire upstairs." An armoire! Yes, and an ottoman. They would have been speaking Venusian to Lucille, they nearly were to me.

"Well you know Steph: the reigning *diva* of fashion. Here, let me pour you some tea while she makes up her mind between ecru and eggshell." She gave out a smile that buttered up the whole room. She would have been Cap's age when she'd met him, thirty-five or so right now and as trim and effusively energetic as her daughter, though the crazy pixie quality I loved in the younger woman (and thought of as "madCap") had been tempered here to what I can only call an impression that hijinks lurked below a sheeting of grace. She wore a tasteful understated gray cotton shift, and not the low-cut high-slit flounce-bosomed sequinney sheath I'd spent my teenage years imagining, but she filled it with motion that was, in every minimal swivel, desirable.

I wanted, out of loyalty to all of my nineteen years and all of Lucille's chopped liver, to hate this winking Tabby set by fate in my path, but that fuddy-duddily noble emotion was doomed by her first, high, musically chimed-out "Steph! How delightful! and—look, you've brought a friend!" I was wowed, I was wooed, I was nineteen years of testosterone putty she could have wanted to gouge out to be deviled eggs for all I cared. I was bought, in a snap. I wanted to live on Venus.

We talked. It couldn't have been more than fifteen minutes, that one and only time I saw her, while Cap deliberated over her scoopnecked mankiller trousseau. "So, tell me about *your* mother." My mother had just been diagnosed as someone whose own cells were greedily eating her away. "Oh, you know, she's fine," I said.

Lucille never came up as a topic. I never received the inkling that any of eighteen years of dalliance in these rooms meant even eighteen minutes of shame felt. Yet I understood implicitly, too, that Lucille was never mocked here. She wasn't a poison requiring Tabitha as an antidote. Tabitha wasn't *against* Lucille—she simply *wasn't* Lucille, period, not in the sheen of one molecule.

Lucille poured tea from a squat, sort of tuber-like, samovar thing. Here, Tabitha lifted a shapely-waisted swan-necked piece of deco-ware, and that was that, and said everything. Which was fortunate; I'd run out of conversation. Minutes later, Cap and I were running out to *Rosie-O's*, as naturally as if I hadn't just dogpaddled time in the place I'd devoted vast swatches of my childhood to Noschelizing wildly.

I could never tell him. He'd have shattered like a dropped 45 rpm. So I protected him from that evening. Or was it merely I was ashamed to have kept "his" Cap a secret from him all along, and by now it was too late to admit I'd entered a new realm of being? In either case, Noschel certainly understood, as did I, that our earlier tether had thinned. I thought of a paper strip you'd find across a motel's toilet seat: a child's pinky could sunder it. In fact, that afternoon we exited Schaumley's beginning astronomy class was the last real time we spoke. Oh, there were a few stiff pleasantries traded through the rest of that semester. But the last truly meaningful words we exchanged were that day. Some pretext allowed itself into existence, we quarreled—I believe we were delighted for the excuse. I had life to get on with.

And I remember now, too—we weren't called out because of

an uproar at Noschel's home. That final confrontation happened a year before; and after nearly two decades of gripes and suspicions, Lucille hired a natty lawyer, who subcontracted a seedy detective, and following numerous months of hyperbolic back-and-forth, her husband was free to bimbo-up his days as richly as alimony allowed him, and as openly as any American happiness could be legally pursued.

No, we were called out—*I* was called out—because of my mother. The doctors saw it waiting darkly an hour or two away. I asked Noschel would he come too; I was shaking. He nonchalantly refused, though maybe the direness wasn't clear: he'd never kept a vigil at the bedside of somebody dying. "Well, jeezus, don't have a fucking conniption fit." He'd been hurt, I think, by my recent burrowing into myself, and now he was hurting me back. We had words, we hollered while the Dean's aide stood there laconically and the couple of hours left to my mother ticked by. Bad words…they come back to me, now.

But what comes back strongest is maybe a month before that, drunk, a doozy of a drunk from a night of rubbing against the loveliest eggshell-or-ecru-gauzed woman at *Rosie-O's*. We've come to her apartment, she's lost for once in sex-exhaustion, but I can't sleep. I've been at the bimbo's that day. I've chatted below her row of Calder, Rauschenberg, and Warhol prints; one is faintly erotic. I think of Lucille, sitting in her brocade chair with an ancient, Stonehengian patience, under the photographs of Noschel sporting his toddlerwear. "So," I say to the bathroom mirror, "now *I'm* Itzie. I'm the monster now."

6.

Where the streets met the river, they twisted.

Slitting the throat of an infant's corpse is easy; finding one, slightly more difficult.

Yes, but the beautiful cut you can make…! It was dead by a day. A cut like the opening into a pocket, trimmed by bluish lavender piping on cream cloth.

Even so, the soft sound sickened him. Oh, you can hear it alright, like slicing into a sack of day-old barleyblock. Now he was here with the thing in his keeping, clucking his wagon into a carefully unremarkable pace toward Jewtown.

Dark already—the air against his cheeks like the wings of a jackdaw. *Ach!* and the burning itch was beginning again, a spider on fire dancing deep in his codpiece. What a day, what a day. His contact in the Old Town, the Staré Mesto, hadn't shown, had left him standing in a street of October mud. And then his contact in Malá Strana, the Little Town, shrugged and held up empty hands.

So finally Brother Thaddeus himself was required to be not only author of this plot, but a supporting participant. Down he'd come from his grove-surrounded building on the Street of the Dominicans—"the green monastery," people called it—and in the relative secrecy of Gallows Hill, one mile and two hundred yards from Niestaedter Gate on the Vienna Road, had handed over the common wicker market-basket. Not a word was exchanged.

So now it was up to him, to Ladislaus Havlicek!

It had looked so tiny, wrapped still in its velveteen, the fingernails as dainty as a courtier's pastilles.

He had his sequence. First he gutted the pig. Without a new breath or wiping the blade, he made his slit in the hardened infant throat. It was only about the size of—what? a loaf of oatcake? Then he wrapped it in the *tallith*, the silken Jew prayercloth, wrapped it exactly the way he'd been shown, the way he would leave it propped in the cellar of Meisel's house: with the grayish-green face peeping out. And then, for discretion, he bundled the thing in the gaping lips of the pig's eviscera-hole. So easy. Drinking a little, waiting for night.

It had died, he saw, of the spotted typhus—*fleckfieber.* He was no murderer. He was... what was he? A deliverer, like hundreds in the city, on the wharfs, at the wooden gate of the Palace, over the great stone bridge's sixteen arches. He said it repeatedly into his cups of Mosel: the only blood on his hands was a pig's.

The tavern part was good—The Crested Mare. He'd had the first of his florins from Thaddeus's man, and it did for a skinful of Rhenish. Then the bawd named Jadwiga recommended toppers of Mosel, and played with his root a bit, trying to jiggle up some business, but his body would have none of that. The sun going low. The wagon out back with its bundle tethered under the rough-woven fisherman's cloth. He'd left when the fiddlers struck up "Go High and Go Low." "You come back later," she tremoloed after him, "my rosy-rose here is for pluckin'." Maybe he would. Maybe he'd like to pass her the burning itch, like one taper leaning into the wick of another... Later.

Now it was dark, but simple dark wasn't enough for unloading this wagon. And now it was pit-dark, up-the-arsehole-dark, good people everywhere digesting the last of their strudel crumbs and readying for sleep. He was in the tannery block, two pegs of its stench in his nostrils... A porter, you could tell by the sign of his trade, a rope around the waist, trudged past... Some carriage from one of the upcountry castles... Sounds, far off, of ale-stained roisterers... Yes, he would go find nasty Jadwiga again, and have her scrub out her little pink changepurse, and then he'd...

A hand grabbed his throat. From behind. He was down in the dirt, his gutting knife was out, *zhht* missed in the darkness, *zhht* he saw he scored a gash in his attacker's forehead, nothing to stop him though, where was he now, *where are you you gooseprick,* and then from the utter black zero of the air the porter's rope cinched his arms to his sides in a single smooth and painful move.

He thought he'd die there, at the hands of this impassive giant, snapped at the neck like a rabbit dinner and all for a few crappy florins, but no. They rode in silence, the giant at the reins, and Ladislaus rattling in back. The fisherman's cloth had been loosened. What was under it rolled from side to side. Ladislaus, on top of it, rolled from side to side. He'd moved his bowels in fright.

He couldn't tell where they were going, he couldn't tell where they stopped. A teetering of the wagon, running—the giant had left. And then guards of the city watch were all around him, untying him, jabbering in their blunt way. He was directly outside their quarters. He was relieved—*was* he relieved? Not jabbering, whispering now.

One of them was delivering an infant from between the spread-open legs of a pig, as carefully as a midwife. It had silken wings.

$$\sim$$

You understand, yes? The Golem, he had been watching all along in his disguise you would call it, and now he leaves this wagon with the policemens, for a proof there was a plot against the Jews. They see the baby, in the *tallith,* in the pig the filthy animal, so they question this man, he says Brother Thaddeus pays me money to do this wicked thing, I was going to put this baby in the Jewish person's house.

"*To plant it there!*"

What, it should grow?

$$\sim$$

The kitchen noises woke him. Pereleh and the serving-girl Rachel, platters stacking, even the quiet shred of carrots being grated. His head hurt. The wine. The wine had softened his head. Another carrot from the kichen exploded inside his skull.

Oh, but it had been in a good cause. Friendship. And a blustery smudgy friendship, that allowed his keeping silent on matters best kept so. Weren't they quite the pair, this Khyto and Pekler—no, no, the other way—these fellow seekers of his. Their nightly looking was foolish, of course: the planets weren't pinheads for fixing the Lord and his Empyrean like a butterfly. Still, they were seekers. Their brains were filled with more than just the price of cabbage. Also…

"*Mein Gott!* Yehuda…" Pereleh entered the room. Since sun-up, she and Rachel had wrestled a fresh catch of twenty-pound carp from a row of the large wooden pails, the *dzber*, the fishermen floated behind their rafts. Now this. It was the first time she'd looked straight at him since his very wobbly middle-of-the-night return.

"What, what?"

"You don't know? Feel! Here," and she took his hand like that of a child learning the names of body parts.

A thin gash over his forehead. It felt as if it could have been made with a *rodel*, that little toothed wheel they use to score the lines in *matzohs*.

"You drink, this happens."

"No, I…" he stroked it in bewilderment. This hadn't happened at Tycho's, he was sure. The carriage ride home was a blur, but…

"Sometimes, Yehuda. What gets into you?"

What gets out?—the thought came from nowhere. And then the breathless voice of Abraham Mintzkhop, the sexton, as he rapped at the jamb. "Rabbi, have you heard the news from the guardhouse! Rabbi, Rabbi Loew!"

~

Quoting Lyall Watson: "One recent survey of over sixty different cultures showed that all but three of these accepted the idea that some part of the personality is independent and can travel beyond the bounds of the body." He lists a number of tribal and shamanistic beliefs; for instance, the African Azande "believe that everyone has two kinds of soul, one of which leaves the body when we are asleep. This *mbismo*, it is said, travels widely, and has all manner of adventures. It keeps these, however, to itself. We have no memory of them on waking."

Enough of his intriguing instances come as well from Western culture, even Western scientific study. No one knows what it means when a man under observation at Duke University says his spirit is leaving his body from where it rests, not sleeps but rests, in a soundproof control room; what they do know is, a half-mile away, a kitten has been confined in a large wooden box and wanders it, meowing, unhappy, only "twice during the 40-minute observation period he stops moving and sits motionless for two minutes at a time," the exact four minutes in which the subject, at the other end of campus, claims to be "out." This is not coincidence; it can be, it has been, repeated on request.

Nobody knows, but there are the many thousand case histories, poltergeists, astral projection, William Travis who, trapped underwater in scuba gear, "in the cod-end of a trawl net," insists some "me" slipped from his body, advising the panicking "other" alongside on how best to saw its way out from the netting.

"I have trouble with souls and disembodied spirits…(but) the survival value of an experience that can save life, is beyond dispute."

And Chayim Block says, in his book of Golem tales, "Some

regarded the Golem as a spectre of Rabbi Loew."

7.

Wft wft wft.

His "real name" was Armando Catalano, but we knew him as Guy Williams, and from October 10, 1957 to July 2, 1959 (two seasons, thirty-nine episodes each) we knew him better as Don Diego de la Vega, and best as Zorro, "the fox."

The October 1958 cover of *Walt Disney's Magazine* neatly captures the premise: Don Diego, ineffectual playboy and idler, gazes languidly into a mirror that reflects (to his own mind's eye, one supposes) his other self, his hero self, the dashing black-masked-caped-and-hatted vigilante Zorro, "the fox so cunning and freeeee," as the themesong reminded us weekly, "Zorro, who makes the sign of the Z!" *wft wft wft* with a rapier-grace the kids in my neighborhood duplicated pathetically (often disastrously, for the nearby vase or younger brother's head) by broom or yardstick.

So we understood the concept of a secret avenger, Noschel and I. The Golem wasn't news to us.

Plastic Man was "really" converted hood Eel O'Brian, who deftly maintained his image as a two-bit thug, the better to take the naked pulse of mobsterdom and so enable his alter-ego's solo, superpowered crusade against crime. (And *quite* a superpower, you might recall: his body could stretch like some industrial putty, clutching hooligans with a reach sleeked out for two or three city blocks—the famous "long arm of the law"—or becoming a living slingshot-band of size enough to carom a boulder. "B'gorra! Skizzle Shanks and his mob!" The cops couldn't hunt them down, but suddenly CRASH! they're packed and delivered through the stationhouse window, held in the rubbery grip of—"That arm! Like a tentacle!!")

By day, "flirtatious fun-loving socialite Marla Drake"; by night, Miss Fury, sexily athletic defender of righteousness, in her skintight black leopard attire. (Was there a tail? I don't remember. There was a half-face mask complete with feline ears, though: fetish costuming for the twelve-year-old.)

If the weekly lesson in Sunday School said any tattered beggar at the door could be an Angel of the Lord (and my memory-centers, urged insistently enough, will yield that black-and-white etching of Abraham magnanimously opening his tent-flap), the savvily merchandised version assured us any splay-eared drip-nosed Noschel-or-me might split like a chrysalis, giving radiant egress to that champion we felt roiling inside. Captain Marvel was pintsize newsboy Billy Batson; we all knew that.

And if Rabbi Loew sent the Golem, disguised as a gentile porter, to loiter in the twisted streets of Prague, to blend with the bricks, to be the espionage deployment of his people…didn't Don Diego send his servant Bernardo to town on similar missions, truly a mute but only deceptively deaf, and many's the time the suspicious Sergeant Garcia would suddenly trigger a blunderbuss in back of Bernardo, hoping to startle him into self-betrayal, but Bernardo continued unloading the coach or picking the jonquils unperturbed, and later reported some evil new machination of El Capitan's to Don Diego, via impassioned hand signals…

We wouldn't know it then—we would have been shocked to discover it then, to have this fictional world's internal logic deconstructed—but the studio used four different horses as Zorro's black stallion Tornado. *That* we didn't need to know, to learn the lessons: No identity was singular. No body out there, but it interconnected somewhere with ally or nemesis.

It grew complex, even in kidville. The July 1965 *Superboy* features a story in which "shy, timid, milksop Clark Kent," strained by exposure to Kryptonite, gives weird vent to his jealousy of his own superhero identity. He builds a lifesized Superboy puppet—it's dressed in the famous robed costume, Clark ventriloquizes its voice—and this he keeps in the basement, slaps around, and psychologically bullies. The puppet appeals to Ma and Pa Kent for help, "Mom, Dad... don't let Clark hit me any more," and they think it best to "play along": "Clark...Superboy...Please don't fight...It's time for dinner! Come upstairs!" There, the puppet justly complains, "But Mom! I asked for steak and french fries!" Clark interrupts with a bang on the table: "I'm giving the orders around here! And I say you're eating ham and eggs, just like me...see?" Clark "snaps out of it," but only after symbolically killing the dummy. A remarkably dark and accurate exploration for a comic book in those days.

In a way, it isn't less complex than Conrad, and prepared us—though "The Secret Sharer" textures and teases its sense of *doppelgängerness* dimensionally beyond the range of the Ma and Pa Kent home in Smallville. College could have been seen as a deepening of the theme I'd glimpsed more thinly, sitting rapt at Lucille's feet. Sometimes the pairing was external: Don Quixote and Sancho Panza yinning and yanging across their windmill-strewn, eventful plains. Sometimes, internal: there's a strikingly-rendered cover to my sophomore lit course *Dr. Jekyll and Mr. Hyde* that shows both personalities clarifying themselves, and what we see is something like a human head in mitosis.

We could grind out half-an-hour's blather in Cinema Studies, over freeze-framed moments of that knowing scene in *Frankenstein:* the doctor and his monster stare at each other through a revolving mill wheel (its blades not unlike a reel of film themselves, just slow enough to make us conscious of the process), and the camera's alternation of those faces that wear exactly the same expression melds them for us. In Art, Rosetti's *How They Met Themselves:* a couple comes upon their mirror-beings (but which is which?) in a woods.

I remember especially vividly Biology's textbook diagram of "the two halves of the brain," as tidily cleft as Cap's two handfuls of butt. "The right side, which lacks the power of speech, often shows more 'primitive' and violent traits, while the left side, which controls speech and writing, generally shows a more creative and rational disposition. They intercommunicate through the *corpus callosum* (see arrow 17). Sometimes, in malfunction, they come into conflict; a patient was caught attempting to choke his wife with his left hand, and all the while his own right hand was witnessed battling against it in her defense."

And so it wasn't difficult to carry this to the cylinder seal impressions illustrating a unit of World Mythology: Gilgamesh, the urbane King of all of Uruk, is wrestling the wild man Enkidu, the hairy and speechless Enkidu, who eventually the King will subdue "and then they were as brothers," but for now the ancient craftsman fashions them fronting each other, hand to hand, in equipoise. I knew: they're even older than Sumerian. They're born in us from back where the brain is as knobbily-veined and pungent as a stilton.

What were syllabi, but blueprints of a balance-pans world? The Raw and the Cooked. The Sacred and the Profane. The I and the Thou. "There is an anecdote, that Shelley met his double walking a terrace. It halted the poet and sternly asked, 'How long do you mean to be content?'" Or quoting from Eliade: "I shall cite as an example the usage made by the Kogi... The tribe is divided between the 'people from above' and the 'people from below,' and the village, as well as the cultic hut, is separated into two halves. The world is equally divided into two halves, determined by the sun's course. Furthermore, there are many other polar and antagonistic couples: male/female, right hand/left hand, warm/cold, light/darkness, etc. These pairs are associated with certain categories of animals and plants, with colors, winds, diseases, and, likewise, with the concepts of good and evil. The good exists only because the exil is active; if the evil would disappear, the good would equally cease to be. The guiding principle of human behavior is *yulúka,* 'being in agreement,' 'being equal,' 'being identified.'"

By then I could bring this binarian library back to the books of my childhood, enlivening both. In 1961, when I was thirteen, Donald Duck, his Uncle Scrooge, and Huey, Dewey, and Louie, visited Valhalla, a mystery planet that abruptly occurred in the skies, and "its magnetic force is equal to the Earth's, which is why the two planets don't crash together." (The magnetic balance gets zapped out of whack, and the planets are set on a pellmell path to smithereens, though our canardian fivesome finally readjusts these lethally undone orbits.)

I would have been a touch older, late in high school or early in my college career, when Tarl Cabot appeared in the first of what would be twenty or more softcore s/m sci-fi adventures set on the planet Gor, to which, as I remember, he was kidnapped. Chapter 10 of the fourteenth volume, *Fighting Slave of Gor,* gives some of the flavor; it's called "I Find Myself Slave in the House of the Lady Tima; I Am Recreation for the Lady Tima, After She has Finished her Work." (I wouldn't say it was better than the ducks, but it provided me assuagements they could never.) Gor was a planet of violence in primary colors, kinky erotic encounters, jewels, chains, eagle-like steeds men flew on, evil priesthoods, telepathic warfare, raw Sinbadian grandeur... Gor was "Counter-Earth," precisely (and undetectably) on the other side of the sun from us.

We're back at Philolaus, aren't we?—1966, Astronomy 101. Two boys in an auditorium, with a "Central Fire" sketched on its board.

I'll tell you: we've archeologied down to his day again. We've walked among those utterly alien columns. Ancient Greece is another planet—yes, but *in this* planet.

One last class: an Ice Age shaman (we assume he's a shaman) is wearing the mask of a stag, or maybe that's the actual head of a dead stag on his shoulders. Maybe it's fairest to say a stag has been given a human torso, it's drawn so smoothly, it's such a seamless and incomprehensible joining of powers. He's lifted some wand, a sceptre or simply a withe he scores the air with in his ritual dancing. Wft wft wft.

~

It's all so far away from me now. It drifts back in like dust from distant sawing—a powder, a polleny piling-up in corners. It may be thick, but collecting it into recognizable shapes again is nearly impossible labor. I'm forty-two. Why bother? Owls need the bones of mice in their guts, to digest. Let the Earth stir her dead. Let it all go on—as it will—without my fussing.

Still, I'm writing this. I'm leaving Skyler's side at 3 A.M. to hush downstairs and jumble words around. Sometimes I even leave the words, and walk outside as if the moon might fit me like a helmet inside which, thoughts grow lucid, thoughts will school like new-spawned fish, their tiny bones as clear as a diagrammed sentence.

Nothing happens much. Fish...helmets... And I finally return to Skyler's side, her sleep-breath in and out like a latch being tested. She isn't any part of this story, I suppose that's the point. We have our own life (as Eliade says) with *colors, winds, diseases, and, likewise, with the concepts of good and evil.* I stretch, I arrange myself alongside her...

Double-entry ledger columns, hoping we add up to love at the end.

8.

That next night, Tycho returned from Baron Rosenberg's banquet doubled over in pain, his face the color and sheen of hamfat. He'd needed to urinate during the meal, held back while his body strained to accommodate this abstemiousness, and now all of Castle Benatek held its breath while he bellowed, and sometimes fought for strength just to bellow. "Bring me that jittering capon," he wheezed.

And so Kepler was led to his chamber. "Don't let me have lived in vain"—the words were bubbles riding a gurgle. Smears of marmaladed hummingbird breast crisscrossed the covers, and there was a linen of coughed blood. Kepler nodded politely, then backed out (nodding the while: *idiot,* he hated himself for that) and felt the scoff breach out of his stomach-waters as soon as he entered the hall. *Ah, such pathos!* —as if some infinitesimal waft of discomfort were really going to carry this behemoth away.

Within a week the Dane was buried in the Teynkirche in Prague. The banker of stars was dead. The key to his vaults was handed over to Kepler. Now the work, the *real* work, the visioning of the span and the beams and the newel, the deciphering of the rings-in-rings of the solar family—now it could begin.

Richard Grossinger: "He alone of his contemporaries was resourceful enough to discover the actual laws of the movements of the planets. His insights were far more radical and sustained than those of Copernicus. He did not understand gravity, inertia, or centrifugal force, but his laws contained everything needed to derive them. If there is one astronomer whose work marks the watershed between the ancient occult system and the modern scientific one, it is Johannes Kepler."

If there is one astronomer, there are two. Colin Wilson: "Kepler began by thinking in terms of idealized shapes; and without Tycho's observations he probably would have continued to do so for the rest of his life. If Kepler had died before he met Tycho, his name would now be unknown."

Looking up from his intricate tables of vectors and ellipses that will illustrate *Astronomia Nova*...something, call it a chill, a memory, running through him...

What the old Jew had said.

~

"Wolf-person! Wolf-person!" Anyway, that's how it translates. Spreading in panic through the streets, and around the small open stalls of the market.

Kepler didn't hear. Or heard, but it was background static, little more than a field of flowers against which the beloved stands out shimmering and radiant. He was carrying *Astronomia Nova*— his beloved—attempting avoiding all dog-piles, puddles, children out playing at stick-and-hoop. He was sorry he'd decided to walk. The folio was wrapped in white lace, and he really did feel as if he were bringng his bride to the Emperor Rudolph (that was his ultimate destination) for approval. (And, with luck, for payment of 2,000 florins of salary the Emperor owed him.) Children were screaming but here, near the ghetto, children or fish-bucket vendors were always screaming.

In those days, tales of infants abandoned in the forests and raised by wolves (or stolen by wolves and raised) were common. So were itinerant beggars and these, appearing from nowhere, smuttied, sometimes crazily violent, were often thought to be beast-people wandered in from the caves. "Wolf-person," then, was a catchall name for anyone running about berserk. These were not good times; you'd hear it yelled frequently.

But Kepler didn't hear, no, he was humming the songs of the stars in his head, he was counting the coins in his future.

When the giant man appeared, he seemed to be flinging off people the way a dog might shake itself of water: two vendors hit a wall and then were motionless; a burly fellow the girth of an imperial cavalryman went flying, one of his arms at a plainly unnatural angle. Everywhere, pandemonium: wailing, animal squawks, snapped wood. Kepler instinctively weighted down his folio under a grain sack, then his instincts, used up, failed him and he stood in the open transfixed.

No wonder: the giant looked as if light streamed from him in jagged pieces—as if, when he stomped through the light, it shattered, like crockery. He growled, he upwrestled a crude bench meant for the seating of six and tossed it with one hand. Then he was right by Kepler, with that same hand raised. The astronomer fell to his knees. He knew the secrets of the fires of the universe, and here he was going to die like some shit-picking beetle mashed into the dirt.

Except—a heartbeat's-length of look, the giant gave him; one could see it as *recognition*, how a foaming dog still passes by a child it had played with once before.

And then the locus of wailing and puke-fear followed the giant elsewhere, left this circle of wreckage to silence, to scouring out the stains, the folio unwedged from its hiding, the sourish sweat being dried by the air, the breezes feathering-up the sun-touched ruff of the river, the planet spinning along its ellipsis— yes, its orbit was an ellipsis now—and the cosmos smoothly interlooping its comets, its brain waves, its maggots and seraphs, *hallelujah,* every thready instance of its infinite tracks.

⌒

Quoting Lyall Watson: "The eldest boy, about eight years old, screamed and dropped his cup. The back of his right hand began to bleed from fresh punctures that suddenly appeared there in a semi-circle, like the mark of a human bite, but with a diameter larger than his own."

This is from Watson's eyewitness account of a poltergeist experience. They are, he says, "by no means uncommon. Alan Gauld, a psychologist at the University of Nottingham, has made a fascinating survey and computer analysis of 500 cases—which he says were not difficult to find. Major breakages and injury occurred in around 10 per cent of his cases, animals were disturbed in 6 per cent, and another 16 per cent involved some kind of assault—invisible pinches, blows, scratches and bites—on human beings."

Of Pierre Janet's studies of multiple personalities, Watson says "that once such a sub-personality is released, it tends to define itself more and more clearly as a separate individual—even to the extent of denying the existence of the first."

Children rebel. So do colonial populations. It could be all creations need to rebel, that any life or pseudo-life tends to evolve toward autonomy. Institutions. Cancer.

Exorcism of *some* kind—de-creation—we see is a cultural constant. The therapist's couch. The silver crucifix. Superboy needed to "kill" the dummy.

~

Brother Thaddeus was ordered unfrocked and sentenced to prison. For many years the Jews were untroubled by false accusations.

On *Lag-B'Omer* of the year Jewish Calendar 5353, the Rabbi Loew commanded Joseph Golem to sleep that night in the garret of the *Altneuschul*, the synagogue. The Golem's sleep was always an even, unbroken thing; and the few dreams in his head were the easy child-like shapes that shells or pebbles leave in clay.

While the Golem slept, and the Jews of Prague slept, the Rabbi and his two attendants climbed the garrret stairs—Isaac and Jacob, who had been with him at the beginning, they were here now. They worked by two candles. They did everything in re-verse. They walked their seven circles in reverse; and they bowed in reverse to the four directions; and the Psalms and the *Zirufim* and the words from the Book of Creation, these were said backwards.

And when they were done, they were standing about a rough clay sculpture—nothing more than that, though dressed in a shirt. And then they covered it with old prayer robes, and thousands and thousands of leaves from discarded prayer books, things that were stored in the garret. Then they solemnly made their way down again—a friend, in a sense, was dead—and washed their hands and chanted prayers of purification, as a Jew usually does after being near a corpse.

Joseph had gone away, the Rabbi told his people. And to climb into the attic of the *Altneuschul* was forbidden on pain of excommunication.

He had often walked alone through the ghetto, meditating. Now he was known to go off by himself for long walks on the city outskirts, watching the sun deposit its cuplets of warmth in the waves of the Moldau, watching the river make its gray way through the ruddy-gray clay banks.

$\sim$

AND (she would always end in histrionic declamation) the Golem is STILL THERE. He waits, if bad peoples come to do no-good, THEN (*beat, beat, beat*) again he'll be alive, a wilgilante.

"Yeah but…"

Go away, play now, you noodles.

~

"...twenty years. And why I'm writing you now after these two decades of mutual silence I can't really guess, though I do know I want to apologize. I was an ass at the end, when your mother died, I know that now, I feel two inches high about it, I was so incredibly self-absorbed in sorting out the zillion wafery chips of my own life. But last January Lucille passed on, leukemia, her own blood turned against her and clubbed her to death from inside. Now don't say I'm crazy or maybe I am, but at the *very* end when I folded one wrist over her other wrist and rang for the nurse, I saw you in the room with me, ghostly, and kind of shaking your head with what looked like tenderness. And do you know what her last words were? "At least I'll be with Itzie again" she looked in my damp eyes with her filmy ones and just said it, after all that earlier bitterness and confusion! I guess I should have said, my Dad had passed on even earlier, '76. But I'd lost contact with him, I wasn't any part of the divorce, I didn't show up at the funeral. The truth is, I was afraid I'd meet his son by the other woman. And I didn't think I could face that. Anyway big guy, I figured I'd drop you a line, I hope it ripples in somewhat receptive waters. We haven't spoken since—Do you remember? Walking out of Shumberg's astronomy class the final day of the semester, with something about ol' William Herschel in chalky squiggles over the board, and a hundred students crazy to get out into the fresh air, and you and I sort of trading sheepish goodbyes and melting into separate parts of the crowd. Guess what, I *am* an astronomer now! Or what I probably should say is, I compile boring research data-bank materials for the observatory. I hear you're a professor and married (a second time?) or so the grapevine says. Do you remember…"

I fold it back into neat thirds. I remember.

〜

It ends, for my purpose, with Sir William Herschel—wandering numb with discovery in the mazy afternoon light of his garden. The year is an even 1800, yes an even two hundred years since the moment Kepler first slunk into Castle Benatek. The text is *Investigation of the Powers of Prismatic Colours to Heat and Illuminate Objects*. The author is colourful too.

I have no need to belabor the list of accomplishments that started for this (then-amateur) astronomer with his first two hundred painstaking attempts at grinding his own telescope mirrors. That list is legend: discovering Uranus, discovering moons of Uranus, discovering moons of Saturn, helping discover (and creating the term) the asteroids…it goes on, as it should go on, coming as it does from a long life lovingly spent in long looking. He was not a theoretician, but a traveler of the night sky, in the most refined of vehicles the age could offer: his own William Herschel-made telescopes. With these he witnessed, with these he adored, "myriads of worlds springing up like grass in the night."

For my purpose, though, I'm emphasizing the man who first recognized binary stars. Richard Grossinger says that Herschel "estimated the periods of revolution of double stars and put into the public imagination the idea of worlds with two sunrises, twin shadows… He realized that double stars were not merely twins because they lay in the same line of sight. They orbited about one another and were physically part of the same system."

And so it makes good imagistic sense that this is the man to discover infra-red, to see that Earth has a twin planet: Infra-red Earth. Can we imagine him?—bumbling to bed with the pulsing conceptual nimbus of infra-red all about him. In his garden: an infra-red garden! A planet the bees see! Secret grottoes of light we enter and exit, yawn through, hanging Babylonian gardens of light, Alhambian pleasure gardens of light, small vegetable plots of flaming everyday haloes we're blind to and don't have a cane...

There are so many things to consider, so many things...the aether, the yonder, the steady-state flux. Though for now there's a cut-crystal glass of his milk, to clear the day's-end phlegm. The glass has a diamonded band around its center, the bedside candle is thousanded there...

Clay-Earth, Light-Earth, Earth and Twin-Earth...

Go to sleep, Old Lensman.

～

Fuckhead.

Another guy honking, slowing down, then tooling around the corner to see if she'll follow and hop in...

Stephanie recognized irony: she was hoofing it to the Plasma Center especially so she *wouldn't* need to peddle her perfect teacup's-worth-of-an-ass to make the rent, and so of course *this* was the morning every yahoo with a dick and a 20 needed to spelunk her. Great.

Not that she'd never peddled it, many years ago, and she wasn't ashamed. In Frisco, after Arnie left. Well, that was then. She was an artist now, she had a show of her neon coming up, she had no time or inclination for those on-the-edge adventures any more, and would these jerkoffs *please* stop pulling up to the curb and rolling their windows down!

Something about this neighborhood. Something about the vibes she gave. Men always saw another her.

Worlds

I.

*J*n 1907 my grandfather landed on
Mars, he'd come so far from his village in Poland. The water lap-
ping the pilings: that was Mars, the wharf itself was Mars, the
mongol rampage of rats was Martian rats that led, by alley
shadows and vats of impossible stinks, to the jammed, flat-broke
and flash-o'-diamonds flush, fat, flammable, wholly contradic-
tory and madcap heart of New York: the capital city of Mars.

A dockside conniver had offered to turn his meager crumple
of Polish paper money into *"'Merica gelt"*—a chiseler bogused-
up in a black silk skullcap.

Here my grandfather stands, some zomboid creature lolling
on the trolley tracks, immobilized by too much Mars too fast.
The trolley's stalled, of course, and clanging at him as if he
were a cow. He's less than a cow. He's a dumbshit Yid, with
Hope and Terror frozen in a polka-step in his breast, and half-a-
handful of chump-change trickling out of his fingers.

⌢

That night he slept beneath an overturned clawfoot bathtub, in a dump behind the warehouse district. At daybreak, when even the garbage shone majestically for a moment, he clambered out, as warily as a hermit crab.

"So. You're Jewish?" A man was standing right there, he spoke in Yiddish. "I come here every morning." He gave the tub a dull kick. "Three days out of four, some greenhorn's spent the night here. Come, you need help?"

He was wearing a black silk skullcap. Once, alright—but not twice: my grandfather threw a loopy punch at his jaw, that he barely sidestepped.

Then, as if he'd practiced this for hours already, the man hunched, swiveled, and neatly tripped my grandfather into a mushy pile of restaurant trash. He held out his hand. "I tell you: come. You need help."

It turned out that he was legitimate—the Hebrew Immigration Aid Society. They walked away, like a father leading his mesmerized son.

And *that* night my grandfather slept in a bed.

⌢

It was one of ten beds in the room, in an HIAS hospice that looked like a caved-in orange crate done up to the size of a boardinghouse. A week, they said he could stay here; not that he even knew which day it was. His nine bed-brethren were already sleeping, filling the dark with their heavy-as-sandbags breaths. An elderly woman had led him here by the skimpiest pinch of candle—now by touch alone he opened his oilcloth sack, removed his pamphlet with the text of the *shachris, mincha* and *mahriv* prayers, and placed it delicately beneath the slab of newspaper meant for a pillow.

At 5 A.M. he leaped up screaming, and ran for a broom in the corner. "G'vald! G'vald!" his roommates heard him shouting, "Geshtroft! Tshepeh zich op fun mir!" (Help! Accursed thing, get away from me!) Watching him, their protector, beat the alarm clock into a pile of springs and glassy powder, until it was stilled.

He had a lot to learn here.

⁓

And he'd prepared, in his nowhere sticks-and-baling-wire village: had perfected his Polish-inflected Yiddish once a week in "immigration class," in the shack out back of Oyzer the cheesemaker's; and had learned "yes," "no," "hey buddy" and the names of seven Presidents starting with Vahsheenktun. But nothing could prepare him for the series of spirit-deadening jobs. He learned why everyone woke at 5 A.M. He learned what they suffered before returning fourteen hours later.

First he became a roller—this meant standing for the whole shift, in a windowless, unventilated room. One day, the draggled end of a day, he did his last cigar and couldn't uncrimp his fingers. After that, he scavenged rags; there was a company that cleaned them in benzene, then trimmed and pressed them. When he worked up to being a trimmer, he was given a space on the fire escape; it was early December, thin snow started falling, and the shop boss wouldn't let him back inside until he'd filled his daily quota. After that, he shoveled horses' shit. The company even brought him out to the race track, it was like getting a promotion: shoveling better horses' shit. "Hey buddy—c'mere." He delivered back-and-forth the envelopes by which races were fixed. He wasn't proud of this; but he wasn't starving.

⁓

By now it's 1911.

"Hey Louie—dipping your dingus lately?"

My grandfather startled up from reading his pulp adventure magazine. He could read—a little. He could shoot the shit with the knock-about guys—a little. Even so, a kind of shameful concern was written over his knobby features. Here they caught him galloping over the novelette-length Wild West, but once again he didn't even know the local argot, from the corner of Forman and Hester.

"Louie, Louie, Louie," with a pitying nod of his richly-pomaded temples. Then he made the little universal sexual mortar-and-pestle sign with his fingers. "Louie: getting any?" A wink, a manly clap on the back.

They were at Jake's, the candy store—the traditional rough-neck hangout. In a neighborhood of rougher necks than Jews', it would have been the pool hall. Here you wouldn't go to find the rabbi, or the penny-a-page *bar mitzvah* tutor: no. The shoeshined streetwise congregated here, the wisenheimers and two-bit rack-eteers, the Jewish cabbies and tough-stuff welterweight prizefighters, even a big ward boss's sharp-creased, pinky-ringed vizier.

Hello Mister I-Own-All-Of-Forman-Street, thought my grandfather.

What he said, though, was "Oh—yah, yah, the sex," and grinned sheepishly, and loathed himself for it. But, hey: these were the boys with the easy *mezuma* folded in rhinestone clips, and they were walking their slice-of-cheesecake smiles straight out of these broken streets, on a beam of American moonlight.

And the pamphlet of prayers, of *shachris, minchah, mahriv?* Did its ghost form ever flutter, a transparent moth, among the racks of racing gazettes and copies of *Amazing Adventure?*

∼

"Louie," he said, "don't kid me. I bet you got the hot pants for some little *tsatchkeleh,* right?" He didn't wait for an answer. He poked his finger at the cover of the magazine—a rugged bucka-roo and a supple Indian princess sped their horses over the plains. "You can shovel their shit your whole life, Louie, you listening? Or you can ride one."

Louie wasn't sure what language this was, but he knew he'd better apply himself assiduously to a study of the licorice nibs and jawbreakers.

"Louie, you listening? We got a little job."

⌒

And Louie did have the hot pants. He'd met Rosie at the Sew-ing Sisters Association *balln* (a ball, a dance). She had a solid peasant modesty, when posing at the punchbowl, with her friends; her hair was tied in a bun, as tight as a fist. But she could dip and slink a catty Coney Island dance-step that you'd swear would call down fire from the sky, and *then* she shook out a luscious tumble of frizzled hair. He wanted to swim in that hair, die in that hair, like a salmon.

What she saw in him...who knows? The world is full of smooth-move wooers. Did she understand that knobby face would give a woman something she could hold to?

They were born not more than twenty miles apart. Yes, but they needed to come to America to meet! Can you imagine! Etc. The moon was out, as big up there as a catcher's mitt. He watched her ankles skitter about the shadows of her skirts. They seemed to have minds of their own, like small white creatures in under-growth. He touched her, and she stopped his hand, but she didn't walk away.

"Is nice—yah?" She was looking up at the full, lush, scoop-of-butter-brickle moon. "In Poland, I see this moon. Now here,

I see this moon. Not so much makes from the changes."

"Some t'ings. In Poland, I don't know *you*." This was a major romantic speech for him, and she recognized that.

"Louie, promise me—nobody else, you'll vant?"

"Rosie, Rosie."

"Louie, a name is not a promise."

"Rosie, yah, alright already, I promise."

"A promise lasts, you know this. A promise…" searching for a definition "…is bigger than all of the miles."

"Rosie, I know vhat's a promise, believe me."

What was she reading? his heart? his dick? She took a quick breath and decided.

"Come—my friend Rebecca, her *zaydee* raises chickens, they haff this little room for the chickens." She grabbed his hand. "You dun't mind chickens?"

No, he didn't mind chickens. He wouldn't have minded a herd of mad elk.

～

That night he didn't dip his dingus; she was carefuller than that. But it began, that night. The more they talked, the more they met to sweatily clench in chicken *drek*, of course the more they had in common. Eventually a look across a room was tele-graphically charged. Yet there is no perfect congruity.

There's a panel in one of George Herriman's exemplary *Krazy Kat* comic strips, where Officer Pupp is smitten under the lunar orb, and batting googoo eyes at the Kat. They say, in their Herrimanesque patois: "Ah-h, 'Krazy' I wonder if yon 'moon'—yon 'June moon'—yon 'love moon'—does not suggest something to you?"

"Sure it do 'Offissa Pupp'—chizz—swiss chizz."

∼

Some nights, rolling away from him, she'd peek back at his snoozing gnomish features and be panicked by the *alienness* of somebody not herself, with his own containing skin and hungers. She had always believed you built a future stone by stone. She was practical, she kept a piled list of her grocery purchases and their prices going back to shack-life in Poland, every morning she scoured every fleck from the hall sink. Her three scarves, that were her treasures, she always hung away in what she perceived to be their proper chromatic order.

And he—! A *blonjenkop*, a "lost head," a dreamer. He was forever shlepping the sack in somebody else's tycoon scheme.

She had a brother, Nate, he managed the shop where a silent row of hunched-over Jews ground lenses for glasses. "Shpecka-tickles, Louie," Nate explained, and with his thumb and forefinger made a circle of each hand, at his eyes. "Pree-sɪsʜ-un vork!" And they were booming, too, Louie could see that: orders slopping over the desk (it needed Rosie's touch) and the grinders bent to their wheels and fussy buffing-sticks from just past sunup to dusk.

"But vhere to go from here? Vhat is our ғᴏᴏᴄʜᴜʀ? Louie, ve need someone," and now his arm around Louie's shoulder, "to t'ink big new t'ings, ve need somebody inᴅᴏᴏstrious!" And Nate would splay the fingers of his free hand, slowly arcing it across the air as if, in its wake, the lineaments of a glittering and unstoppable Tomorrow could be seen.

But Louie didn't think he was indoostrious. He didn't really know *what* he was, most days when he woke he barely knew *where*. And Rosie kept mentioning Nate's place increasingly, bringing the topic to bed with them, confusing it with the sweet beast scent of their mutual explorations—a woman whose wants and visions and hillocky, billowy body might have been, for him, the complete relief map of another planet.

~

I mention this now, in 1990, long after my grandfather's yielded bones are gelatin and a calcium cloud, because it explains the trip he took, vacationing away from the city, trying to clear his "lost head" of conundrums. Some of his friends pitched in: a train ticket, first class ("Got you kless number vun!" said Alfie Sprintzer).

This is what did it, finally; this was the straw:

"We've got to start you out small, you understand that, Louie. But this could be a big-time operation."

Jake had gone in back to count a new shipment of jellybeans. He understood when his ears would best be clean of certain talk.

The man who owned Forman Street possessed, and knew he could rely on, a confiding, persuasive voice. That voice, those gesturing hands at the ends of their fancy uptown double-starched cuffs, had won over aldermen down at the Hall. Kid pickpockets basked in that voice, no less than city development entrepreneurs. Now it was Louie's, all Louie's, lotiony and gold.

The plan was simple: they were organizing, and none too soon, the sharpers down at the docks. Louie would be in charge, the captain. All of the fakes out there, the money-changers crying out their "'Merica *gelt!*" and wearing their black silk skullcaps? — they would report to him, to Louie, the maker and shaker, the *alta kocker*, the Kingpin of the Wharves!

He looked down to his magazine cover: the uncomplicated air of the West, with a yee-ha! and a yippi-ai-yay!

~

In 1907 George Herriman arrived in New York, from L.A., with a five-cent shine on his shoes and a dollar's-worth of sketch pads. Yes and by 1912, he was being sent by Hearst himself to do a series of comic slice-of-life reports from west of the Mississippi. He'd been impressed by Herriman's earlier coverage for the *Los Angeles Times*, especially

UNIDENTIFIED AIRSHIP SIGHTINGS
HAUNT IMPERIAL VALLEY
Monster Soars Through Air
Makes Clicking Noise and Carries a Light
Should Salt Be Put On Tail Of This Fly By Night?

with typically Herrimanesque illustrations. Hearst would see that doors were opened, and jaws of importance oiled for talk. All Herriman had to do was — well, react like Herriman, and mail it back for relishment by an eager New York readership.

Hearst couldn't have been more emphatic, and Herriman couldn't in any case have been more eager to revisit the land of butte and Navajo hogan he'd come to love when bumming the rails twelve years earlier, a punk cartoonist wanna-be with inky stars in his eyes. (Well now it's a first-class ticket and six clicking bottles of Hearst's own private-brewed ale.) He'd written, "Those mesas and sunsets out in that ole pais pintado…a taste of that stuff sinks you — deep." (Well now it was: next stop, Arizona!)

And he'd have time, as over half the continent clacked on by, to scratch away at some ideas for this new strip he was going to juggle room for, some time next year. It's night. The side compartment lights are on, a light so yellow it turns his eggshell sketchbook page to saffron. He rolls a smoke, with one hand, from his shirt-pocket pouch of Bull Durham; with the other, he keeps idly scribbling…what does the mouse say now?…then what does the bulldog say?…then Krazy Kat.

~

This isn't the place to insist on the screwball, skew-all genius of that thirty-one-year run of hi-jinks, low-jinks, and oh-so-sly-winks vaudevillian philosophy: I've paid homage to it else-where, as have others more knowing and eloquent than I am, in the history of such stuffs. As Gilbert Seldes said in his banner-raising essay of 1924, *"Krazy Kat* is, to me, the most amusing and fantastic and satisfactory work of art produced in America today. With those who hold that a comic strip cannot be a work of art I shall not traffic." With his lopsided (or, with Officer Pupp a participant, a truly *kop*-sided) triangle (ever-ingenue Krazy; villainous Ignatz Mouse; and Pupp of the local konstabulary), Herriman created a krackpot kosmos that transcended the limi-tations of its form, and became, in all of its antic variety, a single sinuous rhapsody of comic meditation, mythopoetic and simply heels-clicking high-spirited at once.

What I need to mention now, though, is "Herriman's lan-guage, Joycean before *Finnegan's Wake*—the words all working, bouncing, and playing off one another, veering from a bop rhythm to a dazzling poesy. As Ignatz Mouse said, 'Plain lan-guage, but in a higher plane.'"

So says *Krazy Kat: The Art of George Herriman,* and points out that the "alphabet soup" involved here included "Victorian prose, the lowest street slang, onomatopoeia, Spanish, French, the alliteration of Navajo names and"—*mais oui* ("Of cawss you may," the Kat might say, "be my guess")—"the Yiddishized diction of New York's Lower East Side." When Krazy arcs her flapjacks backwards, then *presto* catches them standing on her head, her self-approving comment on her adroitness is "Oy, a trix—fency."

I belabor this because, as the miles rattlingly pass, George

Herriman sits there, doodling, with his lumped-up swayback Stetson hat pushed so far back on his head it's nearly a memory...sits there fascinatedly eyeing this fellow across the aisle, who's reading a richly garish-covered issue of *All-Story,* moving his lips along with the English as if grazing it, stopping every now and then to argue vehemently with the open text, with frequent punctuations as the hero faces imminent demise (or love-hugs): "Oy!" "G'vald!"

~

But when Herriman tapped him lightly on the shoulder and wordlessly offered him a room-temperature beer, my grandfather rose to the lingual occasion. "Hey buddy, man, hokay by me, Mac!" He'd had nothing to eat since Ohio, when the last of Rosie's sandwiches ran out; and there's a Yiddish saying, *Beser toyt shiker eyder toyt hungerik* — Better dead drunk than dead hungry.

Louie raised the sweating bottle to his benefactor: *"L'chayim."* It was gone in four pulls.

So they talked. They shmoozed, they chewed the phoneme fat together long past the world-revivifying rise of the next day's sun. Life. Women. Betting the ponies. Legendary New York dandies. Those airships (after Herriman explained them). Dreams. Death. Dipping the dingus. What's suffering for. The grand themes, newly girded and gilded to match these far-flung temperaments.

Herriman opened his sketchbook gingerly, and my grandfather studied the whole incipient anthropomorphic cast, including Joe Stork and Gooseberry Sprig the Duck Duke. "Don't vorry," he said encouragingly, with all of the friendly largesse he could fit in a smile, "you vork hard, you gonna gets better." Herriman found this a real hoot. "Lou-boy, you tickle my buzzum," he told him.

And later, passing pastureland in the slumbrous touch of the noontime sun—"MOOY!" my grandfather shouted, and in explanation pointed at a cow. And you can see her, lowing out that bovine Yiddishism, in panel 6 of the April 23, 1922 *Krazy Kat*.

⁓

But this is 1912.

Night's circled back again, George Herriman is snoring, and Louie studies the huge, close clockface of a full moon, and the innumerable stars, as many, as painfully lovely, as when he'd look up at the sky from the rural darkness of Poland. Where was he running to *now*, and why? He'd told Rosie he'd write. How complicated does any one life become in always refolding itself?

The Kat will also wander her gaze "among the unlimitless etha." The Kat will also sing a runaway's tune: "Press my pents/ An' shine my shoes/Gimme twenny cents/To pay my dews—/ For I'm goin' far a-waay—/Tidday." But that's still in the future. For now, it's my grandfather, watching the night-black sand, and the nearly touchable desert sky, go streaking through his head he sees reflected in the window he looks out from. It's almost as if he's watching his own brain first inventing these things: the desert, the wheel of the zodiac, such admirable creations… And *his* constellation, The-Stars-Like-Stones-In-A-Chicken's-Gizzard, grinding another night away… He sleeps…

Next stop, Arizona.

2.

"Is The Master Unit ready?"

"No sir. Not yet sir. But…"

"*But?*" Lowell is indignant. Or *can* a person be indignant with

a machine? He shrugs, he loses the prickly edge of his exaspera-
tion. A night is only so long. He has work.

~

He was named after Percival Lowle—and his pedigree is
traceable back unshakably to this nominative worthy who, in
1639, age sixty-eight, in the considerable company of his wife
Rebecca and fourteen others related by blood or business,
boarded the *Jonathan* at London, and nine weeks later arrived at
Newbury, forty miles northwest of Boston.

In general, the Puritan settlers of Massachusetts Bay "were
more affluent, better educated and of a higher social class than any
other large group of colonists who came to America." Their
intention was to establish a society of saints, as an exemplum for
the future, and so their settlement "in the eyes of Puritan lead-
ers…appeared to be the most significant act of human history
since Christ bade farewell to His disciples." Categorizing the
simultaneous settlers of Virginia, Massachusetts Bay Governor
Winthrop dusted off his saintly thesaurus and referred to "unfit
instruments—a multitude of rude and misgoverned persons, the
very scum of the people."

The Lowles were a specialdom even amidst the Massachusetts
elect: "Percival Lowle, Gent." bore the heraldic ensign of knight-
hood (it was the family's since the fifteenth century): educated
richly, he could speak Italian Mantuan, and read Ovid in the original. At twenty-six, he had been Assessor of Lands—an inherited
office—and, later, a prosperous import/export merchant prince.

Not surprisingly, Lowle, with this advantageous background
and his own ambitious savvy, throve in America. He lived to
write a 100-line elegy for Governor Winthrop. He died in 1664,
age ninety-three; from then, unbroken, the family stock continues, privileged, meritorious, nearly sacrosanct: "the Lowells

speak only to God" becomes a common comic trope, and for three generations about the textile town of Lowell, Massachusetts, "Lowell" and "millionaire" are properly synonymous.

In 1854, Augustus Lowell married into another Boston Brahmin dynasty, and his wife, the former Katharine Lawrence, bore three children; Amy, the youngest, the Imagist poet; Abbott, the middle, the President of Harvard; and the eldest, Percival, born in 1855. "I came into this world with a comet, Donati's Comet of 1858 being my earliest recollection—and I can see yet a small boy half way up a turning staircase gazing with all his soul into the evening sky where the stranger stood."

~

And all of this brings us down to autumn, mid-autumn, of 1912. He's at the 24-inch telescope, a man of fifty-seven as straight and staunch all night as a styptic pencil. He's looking. He's in his eighteenth year of looking, of studying Mars in each red flange and dander and follicle. Some nights Mars wants to cloud its face like a flirt, but Lowell won't take no for an answer, not from his own unwavering eye, and not from one of the 70 million miles. He's going to see each crimson pock, and its rim, and its shadow.

Though, in truth, tonight he also has another urgent project on his mind. "Oh Mr. Tolliver...," and in a flash Mr. Tolliver is here. He's the perfect associate for Lowell, almost archetypally so: his greatest passion is astronomy; his singlemost allegiance is to Lowell's maverick theories; his hair is a series of bright gray military cleats. Like most of the staff men here, he's abnormally methodical, and clippish in speech. Tonight he seems more soft than that in his manner, however—abashed, perhaps.

"Mr. Tolliver. Is it functioning yet?" *It* is The Master Unit, a showy telescope with an 84-inch lens, inset with a thermopyle and mounted with a single-prism spectrograph of Vesto Slipher's invention. While the eyepiece is a dainty thing like a jeweler's loupe (and calculatedly so: the Master Unit is intended to woo the favor of a list of high-profile, influential visitors) the barrel is about as big around as a subway tunnel (this is also calculated for effect). The whole thing comes, by various metal waists and accordion pleats, to rest on four diminutive feet, like those of a portable tray-table. Yet the total effect of the massive, levered and socketed main section, is that of a major city skyline tilted upward at the stars.

It's an impressive contrivance, surely; and so it dwindles Mr. Tolliver all the more when he says, "No sir. But we're working at it. We're checking the section relays now."

At this, Lowell snorts—a well-bred snort, but a snort. They've checked the circuits and the beam-struts and the inloads and, with something like thirty-six hours remaining, he doesn't see now why massaging the goddamn section relays is going to do one batshit dash of good.

But all he says, composedly, is, "Mr. Tolliver. Please be aware that the press arrives in little over a day. Some may be…hostile to our position. We are intending to overpower them, you know, by the plain cold facts of it we hope, by bulk and showmanship if necessary." Mr. Tolliver nods, because he knows this, and because Mr. Tolliver always nods when Mr. Lowell speaks, and energetically nods: as if he's checking off a list of orders. "Please, Mr. Tolliver. Have the men persevere." Mr. Tolliver leaves.

And Lowell is alone again, slumped, fuddled for a moment. Over eighteen years he's made of himself a serious, professional observer of the heavens; though he knows he can be colorful, espousing his ideas, he's no sideshow barker. Yes, but with the constant and indeed increasing volleys of rebuke at his ideas…

But then—he *is* Percival Lowell—he squares his shoulders; also, one time, flicks them, as if shooing off a gnat. And now he's back to his looking, back to his ever-finer-resolving vigil, as still, as steady, as a concrete gargoyle set on this bench. No, that's not true: the eye at the lens is alive, is at its task with a ravenous basilisk-fire.

~

And what would Louie have been to this man with the family crest and the white wing collar so stiffly starched it might be bas-relief sculpture? Very little. Less than little. Antipathetically little: unrestricted immigration appalled him; once, at least, he spoke against it at a public forum. My grandfather would have been somebody meant for brooming the floors and freshening the cowbarn hay, if that; and only then, if hired third-hand by a recent office lackey unacquainted with the ambience.

And still I need to praise the Lowell genealogy here, and enable it forward. Not that his marriage at fifty-three to Constance Savage Keith brought any biological issue—no. But in the metaphoric way in which we use the term, he was the "father" (*he* would have disowned them, but he was provably the father) of the Martians (the "Barsoomians" to use the indigenous language) in eleven novels by Edgar Rice Burroughs—and so, unwilling, the patriarch of the sturdy green line of every insect-eyed, antenna-waving, raygun-wielding extraterrestrial from the saucerfied 1950's to date, that ever landed and indicated take me to your leader.

~

And *Lowell's* "father"?—was Schiaparelli. The respected, keen-eyed Giovanni Virginio Schiarparelli. With the usual collaterally ancestral and second-cousin voices offering background provocation:

Bernard de Fontenelle is opining as early as 1686, "The Earth swarms with inhabitants. Why then should nature, which is fruitful to an excess here, be so very barren in the rest of the planets?" Why, indeed!

Huygens writes a volume of speculations on the citizens of other planets. Kant considers that Earth and Mars, as "the middle links of the planetary system," have inhabitants "that stand in the center between the extremes of physiology, as well as morals." The eighteenth-century astronomer Johann Elert Bode, however, computes by a lucid system of mathematical proportions, that the Martians are considerably more spiritual than their counterparts on Earth. "It is the opinion of all the modern philosophers and mathematicians, that the planets are habitable worlds"— Benjamin Franklin in *Poor Richard's Almanack*, 1749.

In 1784, the King's Astronomer, William Herschel, correctly concludes the whiteness visible over the polar regions of Mars is cap ice — going on to guess that the beings of Mars "probably enjoy a situation in many respects similar to our own." (Herschel also believed the sun is "richly stored with inhabitants.") In 1892 the French astronomer (and toast of the town) Camille Flammarion claims "the present inhabitation of Mars by a race superior to ours is very probable." Three years later, the New York *Tribune* reports a scribble of certain dark markings across the Martian surface spell out the words "The Almighty" in Hebrew. Could Mars be attempting a conversation with Earth?

Then don't just revolve around silently! Plans proposed (and often by highly regarded minds of the times) include, for instance, the Pythagorean theorem drawn to half the size of Europe on the wastes of the Sahara (or better: *dig* the theorem, fill these trenches with water, pour on kerosene, and set the theorem gargantuanly on fire); mathematician Karl Friedrich Gauss suggests a *vaaaaast* wheat field, the size of many Rhode Islands, ("wheat because of its uniform color"), shaped to be a right triangle, bordered by pine trees, in Siberia.

It's an age of scientific optimism and mechanical cockiness, writ large. The completed Suez Canal is considered "a wonder of the world," and every day in the press the progress of the Panama Canal is debated. Gods are tottering, and the astronomical jots they leave in their vacated places take on burning meaning. Bricklayers, bartenders, bottle washers: everyone's a dabbler with an ephemeris, and the *wunderdabbler* sons of the rich especially. Lowell brings a six-inch telescope when he travels as a young man to Japan.

In 1893 he returns to the States with this objective: "nothing less than to build, equip, and staff a major new astronomical observatory in the best possible location," to continue the work of the ailing Schiaparelli.

It's now sixteen years since that night in Milan when Schiaparelli witnessed the geometric pattern of lines he properly labeled *canali*. "Channels," it meant, though overnight a world gone hungry for worlds was making "canals" of it—those *engineered* things.

~

He is conquering Mars; and he is Mars's vassal. He is stroking that face like a lover, like a proper Victorian lover, with his gaze alone, from afar. He is the obliging amanuensis, to whom Mars dictates its lines. He is Lowell. He is tired. He is sitting at his bench with the pride of a rajah in his howdah. He is reading the varicose scrabble of that face. He is tired. The night is tired. The deeply-burned lines of Mars are holding it, like a cheese in a net. He is Lowell, he is the sacchadee here, he is going to look, and chart, beyond being tired, what they call "the Red Planet"—yes, that tobasco-glint in his eye.

~

Eventually—and repeatedly—he would see, and exhaustively sketch for his *Annals*, 700 canals: "a mesh of lines and dots like a lady's veil." The astronomical language is lushly evocative at times—"a twilight arc on the terminator," "limblight," "gemination," "albedo and density"—but data was arrived at in a systematic, dutiful shift at the heavens-scanning tubes.

He was indefatigable, and his legacy is as serious as his intent. His early insistence on the importance of atmospheric conditions to findings soon became seminal. His "velocity-shift" technique for spectroscopically determining the composition of other planets' atmospheres became a recognized practice. He was confident a "trans-Neptunian planet" existed, "Planet X" he called it; and the first two letters of *Pluto* stand for Percival Lowell, its harbinger. Under Lowell's influence, Lampland began his attempts at direct photography of the planets, and Slipher conducted his observations of spiral galaxies that enabled Hubble's discovery of the universe's expansion. Lowell, everywhere. Lowell at the lectern, in the headlines, by the elbows of the sky-beguiled.

"The Roosevelt of astronomy," the *New York Times* says, in 1907. (And later, when Pluto had been discovered, the *Times* quotes Keats's sonnet: "Then I felt like some watcher of the skies / When a new planet swims into his ken."—And so Keats enters this essay, a moment only, but he'll be back.) Uranus! Meteor showers! The mysterious rings of Saturn!

But it's Mars on his tongue tonight like the holy wafer, Mars his uncurable bloody cyst. He will helix its skin clean off it, like the sweetest freestone peach. He will devour it like a temptress's cunt. He is Percival Lowell, and this is his Grail. This is his weight, as Earth was for Atlas. This is his weight, he will carry it into clearer understanding. He is Percival Lowell, his telescope is his pool cue, he will strike this ball dead-on and watch the sparks collect in his pocket. He is tired. Sometimes he is very tired. He is its Boswell. He is its weary retiree walking it on a leash of pure vision. Cherry tomato. Pimiento. Slice of cayenne pepper irritating his nights. Sometimes he wakes, he's been scratching a rash across his chest, where his heart is, the color of Mars.

~

He saw the canals.

"Think back on '07," said the *Wall Street Journal*. "What has been in your opinion the most extraordinary event of the twelve months?…not the financial panic which is occupying our minds, but the proof afforded that conscious, intelligent human life exists upon the planet Mars."

He saw the canals, he labored. "Lowell's plan of attack was eminently pragmatic. He intended, in effect, to lay telescopic siege to the planet." In 1907 alone, Lowell and Lampland "obtained 3,000 images" of the Martian disc with their early ratchet-and-squeeze-bulb camera.

He saw the canals, he proselytized: *Mars and Its Canals* (1906), and *Mars as the Abode of Life* (1908). He said, "I believe that all writing should be a collection of precious stones of truth which is beauty." (And so a whisper of Keats is heard amidst the apparatus: Lowell's sister's influence. Amy.)

He saw the canals, he understood the message in their web-work. He said, "It is by the very presence of uniformity and precision that we suspect things of artificiality. The better we see these lines the more regular they look. The intrinsic probability of such a state of things arising from purely natural causes be-comes evident on a moment's consideration. That life inhabits Mars now is the only rational deduction from the observations in our presence. Think of the intelligence and far-contrivance nec-essary to execute and maintain a system of irrigation worldwide!"

He saw the canals, as when a child at Miss Fette's Boston school for the Brahmin heirs, that lady of strict comportment leaned above him with her lavender-gargled breath and said, "This is very charming, Percival, but here where you tell us *I fell down* you employ the word *down* gratuitously: one cannot fall *up*," but he knows better, every night since 1894 he's fallen, helpless Alice, up that wonderland rabbit hole without bottom.

He saw the canals, his namesake Percival Lowle also pioneered "the New World."

He saw the canals, in 1907 the London *Daily News* said, "He is the greatest authority on Mars we have," (the year my grandfather Louie woke up mapping in his travel-baffled head the *drek*-infected streets of the Lower East Side of New York).

"These delicate features," said Percival Lowell. These are the canals, chimeric and none the less quantifiable, for which, in 1894 — in the Arizona Territory, near Flagstaff, in sight of the San Francisco Mountains, on a mesa at an altitude of more than 7,000 feet, in Coconino County, on the Coconino Plateau, "far from the smoke of men"—he built a "fitting portal to communion with another world."

$\sim$

The gods are wind and death and thunder and the buttery slime of birth, the gods are light and perception, light and darkness, darkness and fires-inside-the-flesh.

In 1907 Natalie Curtis published *The Indians' Book*. She says, "At a Navajo healing ceremony in some hogan where there is sickness, the steady rhythm of the medicine-songs pulses all night long. These songs ('Hozhonji songs') describe a journey to a holy place beyond the sacred mountains where are ever-lasting life and blessedness. The Divine Ones who live in and beyond the mountains made the songs…" And made *this* world, of fevered skin and thinning game and corn and wolves and ambitions and spittle and burials and pollen, a world interpenetrable with Theirs.

And for the Hopi, as well, the deific dwells in the mountains. "The Kachinas are somewhat analogous to gods or nature spirits," says Edward T. Hall. "They live with the people for half of the year and return to their home in the San Francisco Mountains (north of Flagstaff, Arizona) for the remaining six months."

Do the Hopi make love? Do they sob? Do they stand on their sandstone mesas, mazily lost in regarding the star-beaded black cloth of night? Of course. And yet their universe is fundamentally *other* from mine. "No past, present, or future exists as verb tenses in their language. Hopi verbs have no tenses, but indicate instead the validity of a statement. Hopi seasons are treated more like adverbs. Summer is a *condition:* hot." There is no word that corresponds to "time," and Hall describes the Hopi as "living in the eternal present."

Now the maidens have gathered wild sunflower petals from the mesa at the lip of the kiva, the underground ceremonial chamber. Now they wet their faces. Now they dust themselves with golden powder ground from the petals. Now the Lagon and Oaqol dances begin... The gods touch our lives: the sky is a membrane. The gods announce themselves: our dreams are a hearing trumpet.

> *Call the Great Ones down from the Mountain,*
> *Call the Great Ones down*
> *From Sisnajinni, from the Chief of Mountains!*

—"communion with another world."

∼

This is the place, the spirit, that moved Herriman so deeply, its presence is verbally homaged and clearly if cartoonily cartouched throughout his other, more daily love: the *Krazy Kat* strip.

"Herriman made many trips into the Indian country of Northern Arizona. He stayed at Kayenta, on the Navajo Reservation, with John and Louisa Weatherill, at the trading post they had opened there in 1910. Through them, Herriman came to know the country in all its moods and facets. *Krazy Kat's* Coconino has the spaciousness and airiness of the high northern desert. In this vast space Herriman places indigenous mesas, buttes, lunatic cacti, tumbleweeds, blue bean bushes, rock formations, adobe houses, shifting and changing like mirages. He scatters pots, rugs and Mexican and Indian decorative devices; the latter even appear on trees, clouds, or other props necessary to his stage. One Sunday page depicts Krazy sleeping next to a traditional Navajo loom, on which she has just woven a 'febric.' 'That's the country I love,' said Herriman, 'and that's the way I see it.'

"He said that when he passed on he and his dogs would roam that place for a thousand years."

~

In whatever atemporal pneuma exists, that holds the populous Native American pantheon in its travel from the San Francisco Mountains to the beckoning of women and men...the Healers, the Beneficent Ones, who hover about the path of the Great Corn Plant (Sun Bearer, Talking God, even little Dontso the spirit messenger-fly, and the rest) are being called by the ancient chants, to the sick boy's side and, having arrived, being immanent now in the world of tooth and salt, they start their supernatural doctoring...

And Herriman has Krazy say, simply: "In my Kosmis, there will be no feeva of discord."

~

"Mars Hill," as Lowell dubbed the mesa. "Site eleven" is what it had been in the earliest days, when he was also considering "1) The desert of Gobi 2) the veldt of the Transvaal 3) the Samoan Islands."

The seeing here, it seems, has always been good.

We know that in 1054 A.D. a supernova appeared "just above and to the left of a crescent moon," as Evan Connell puts it. "European intellectuals failed to report the guest star" but "a pictograph showing a cross with a crescent moon just beneath it and to the right" (datable by potsherds to—correct!—the eleventh century) "was found on the wall of Navajo Canyon in Arizona."

1912. It's dawn. Well, it's a little before: the air along the desert horizon isn't yet touched by light, no, but is emptying itself, by imperceptible gradations, of darkness. Lowell hasn't slept. He loves this moment, when the Earth becomes as real for him as Mars has been, and he packs that latter planet away inside himself like a red corpuscle. Lowell, his 'scopes, his entry books.

We know, we tell ourselves we know, the universe is infinity foliate; nothing should surprise us. Yes, but can it *be*, that the mesa of the Navajo gods, and the telescope-poking "site eleven," exist coeval in space-time, with their separate dreams occurring on this same one physical sandstone x?...

The scholar of Edgar Rice Burroughs's Martian novels, John Flint Roy, says, "Carter's description of the planet differs in some respects from that given by our Earth scientists. Thus, we feel compelled to assume that Barsoom and Mars are not one and the same; rather, that the former occupies the same place as the latter but in another dimension—the Barsoomian dimension."

Seated at home behold me,
Seated amid the rainbow,
Seated at home behold me,
Lo, here, the Holy Place!

Another night of observation is over. Lowell rubs his face, as if his hands were roughly-nubbed towels. A cup of hot tea is waiting for him, and a shaving of Boston rum cake.

〜

"Mr. Tolliver is making a final check just now." It's Langland speaking. His eyes rove toward the door. Beyond it, Tolliver is desperately attempting to placate the obdurate coven of gremlins that are fucking-up The Master Unit. Lampland smiles—Slipher the Elder is to his left, Slipher the Younger is at his right, and they smile as well. But Lampland's voice is a sieve out of which all hope has dribbled.

"Gentlemen. Very well." By now it's full-tilt dawn, though these four men are oblivious to its mercurial silvers and desert tangerines. They're grouped in Lowell's study. He plays with a rumpled telegram on his desk; its greeting peeks out, HAIL. His fingers crease his lower lip. It's like watching an I-beam fidget.

"It may be in the next few hours Fate will reward us with greater luck. For now, however, we best had expect disappointment. You know, of course, our visitors sent from Mr. Hearst arrive at noon. And scheduled for later, at three," and now he glances at the telegram, "my sister arrives on the afternoon Atlantic and Pacific stop…" and he trails off, unsure of what to say. Perhaps they need preparing for this?

"My sister, gentlemen…" Yes? They wait. A look of mingled love and embarrassment suddenly shadows his face. And then he says by way of explanation—he's speaking to three grown men who live alone in a dome in the desert counting planets and stars like fireflies in a jar—he says, as if he were speaking to any middle-class family at its breakfast table, "You should know… My sister Amy is…" almost, he pities them "…*truly* an eccentric."

3.

The President of Harvard University, Abbott Lawrence Lowell, is at his desk. The desk is a fine-grained wonder, about the size of a small-town plaza, and as lustrous as a mountie's boot at dress parade. Even the desktop humidor is expansive, it could coddle a couple of preemies, and its lid is ivory and cloisonné fretted into a Byzantine pattern. From the walls, the money and minds of two generations of stiff-necked Boston patriarchs stare down unblinkingly, stern (if money), owlish (if mind). The phone looks like an obsidian monument, freshly waxed. And the man behind the desk is the man—his every gesture says this: he is a Lowell—who is capable of answering such a phone.

"President Lowell…"

"Yes, Miss Supwich."

"I have a caller here," and Miss Supwich's voice says that this is a call she's accepted the way she might a rotten kipper, by two reluctant fingers with her nose averted, "who claims an emergency. Shall I…"

"Yes. Please transfer the call, Miss Supwich. Thank you."

"Yes sir." *Click. Mmph.* "Go ahead, sir."

"Right. Y'er Mr. Lowell?"

"I am, sir."

"The *Haaahvard* Mr. Lowell?"

"The same, sir."

"Well then. I'm out the Bay Roadway by Lowsley. Rummle. Eb Rummle. I repair cars, and I've jest repaired a Pierce Arrow broke down here early this mornin. The lady driver is a big fat dame who says I should charge the bill to you—she bein your sister. So. Do I have yer permission?"

Let me interrupt this anecdote for a minute. Let's look at that scandalous and battleship-plated woman.

⁓

She was nicknamed The Postscript—Percy's idea. She was the last of five, by a lag of twelve years, so the sobriquet was a natural. Now there were seven Lowells under the roof, and they named the manor in Brookline, Massachusetts "Sevenels." Here she was born; and fifty-one years later, here her ruptured body let go of its cantankerous tank-like ghost.

This was the house of America's home-grown aristocracy, and in its rooms she comfortably grew into her birthright privilege. The private schools. The private coach (the coachman let her hold the reins once she was three). The subsidized publishing of her fairy tales. Lessons at Papanti's, the—no: *The*—young ladies' school of dance in Boston. The European tour (she was eight). At a dinner party, when she was five, Longfellow "carried me round the table in a scrap-basket, and the recollection of that ride is as vivid as though it were yesterday."

The adult who burst from this chrysalis was, not surprisingly, lavish and willful. "To argue with her," Carl Sandburg said, "is like arguing with a big blue wave." The day she stood at the forum to veto retaining a cherished but senile school board member, she was hissed, but she was hearkened to; no other Lowell woman had ever spoken in public before. And when she lectured on "Some Musical Analogies in Modern Poetry," Amy Lowell became the first woman to give a talk at Harvard. Maids were tossed away like matchsticks. Waiters vied in predicting her wants like adepts at the Buddha's side.

Her father died in 1900; she bought Sevenels and began its Amyfication. Chinese wallpaper. Whistler. Monet. Commissioned Egyptian scenes. The sweeping central staircase that was "carpeted in glowing crimson stair-silk woven to order." Every doorknob on the estate was sterling silver. Japanese stone carvings. Persian rugs. Venetian masks. A sixteenth-century crystal chandelier. Enameled snuffboxes (Paris), elfin music boxes (Lausanne). Two huge white caststone lions standing guard at the gate.

Her English sheepdogs (whelped from Ringlow's Sultan, a "champion of record," and Flo) were awarded free run of this rarefied domain; each day these seven ate ten pounds of top-round beef with flanking mounds of fresh mashed vegetables. After dinner, gathered about the fireplace in the library, guests at Sevenels were ritually handed turkish bath towels, as an interceding between their laps and the freely-offered slobber. Her custom-built Pierce Arrow limousine (which we've encountered, waiting repairs by Lowsley) was maroon, and her chauffeur and footman were consequently liveried in maroon to match. Magenta, though, she abhorred, and "no magenta flower was ever allowed in her garden."

She wrote all night, and woke in her third-floor bedroom at two in the afternoon. And then she'd ring a series of bells for the downstairs rooms, beginning the daily Sevenels procession: Ada, her live-in love, with the mail; the housekeeper, bringing a pitcher of ice water; Amy's wardrobe maid; the parlor maid (bearing packages); and the kitchen maid with the breakfast tray. Additionally, the staff included seven undergardeners (watchful, one supposes, for the least magenta interference), a laundress, and the aforementioned blendingly-uniformed chauffeur (or sometimes two chauffeurs) and footman. One biography adds: "A man came weekly to wind the clocks."

This ambience of retinue and particularized itinerary accompanied her on her travels. "She always refused to stay at private houses, but put up at the best possible hotel, where she required a suite of five rooms, in addition to a room for the maid somewhere else in the building. All electric clocks had to be stopped; all mirrors and other shining objects were swathed in folds of black cloth; the housekeeper saw that exactly sixteen pillows, chosen for plumpness, were perfectly set across the royal bed." Once, when the pillows were flabby some gastrically-restless night, "she ripped two of them open, and transferred the feathers from one into the other." On a train to Milwaukee, wanting fresh air, she "made the porter bring and hold a ladder while she clumbered up and broke one of the small glass panes near the roof."

Her ideological luggage was of a piece with this imperiousness. The industrial looms of Lowell, Massachusetts enabled her family's philanthropies. The pattern of her life, in a sense, was woven by the arduous, humpbacked, fifty-four-hour work weeks there; and this, like the seasons, or gravity, was something fit and unquestioned. "Haughty, class-conscious, high-minded," C. David Heymann calls her. She believed the Lowells among an elect "who had the right to carry their coat of arms." She gave up smoking a pipe, in part, because of its association with "shanty Irish women."

Union organizing was in the air, and the Suffragist movement. But Amy Lowell could blithely refer to "the ignorant proletariat." She's on record declaiming "I have no patience with the new-fashioned woman and her so-called rights. I believe in the old-fashioned conservative woman and all of her limitations." She spoke against retaining the maiden name in marriage. Wobblies were monsters. London bobbies were, above all other duties, for hailing her cabs.

Outmoded elevation, her view has become the one poets rally

against. It leaves her with her verses, on a promontory, crooning to the Muses, while the rest of the planet turns willingly back to regarding its inequities and fractures.

She "devoured," one source says, Dickens; "all of Dickens," says another. Presumably she enjoyed, she agreed or she thought she agreed, with Dickens; it's impossible to picture someone finishing those many thousands of tightly-grouted pages as an exercise in argument. Yes, but—what did she think, when all of his smudged and crumpled-up children entered another demeaning day of factory work? when all of those wadded and tossed-away women, nearly bruised to the look of maps, slipped into the night from their laborers' shacks? The mansions of England, like so many termite queens, are clearly being fed by the energies of some of the author's most charming (and most pitiable) protagonists. What *frisson* ran through her, reading these things? What necessary obtuseness keeps a world undefiled by neighboring worlds?

~

She was five, and lonely. Her father was forty-nine, and remote. But Percy, at least, played jacks with her, and lifted her up to pat the row of carved animal heads, or looked in on the dolls made out of chicken wishbones with sealing-wax faces. Compared to the other, stiffer Lowell males, he was streaked with occasional playfulness, and he became a combination idealized-older-brother-*cum*-supervisory-parent (later, her earliest urges toward a published book would be "to emulate and surpass" his *Mars*).

"I dare you!" Percy said at a family party. Amy was eight. She'd zested her way through a giant plate of rice pudding, and now was eyeing a second plate—which also disappeared, and when it was time to leave, her coat wouldn't button across her middle. "And," she wrote, "it never buttoned again."

Oh she was ponderous! At twenty she was barely five feet tall but weighed 250 pounds. Oh she was a ponderous, square-rigged, bunker-built thing!

～

—A glandular, uncorrectable condition. She needed to twist her body when rounding the turns of the spiral stairway. Alice Lowell remembers being a child at a family dinner when Amy barged in "perfectly enormous in a vast gold dress cut tent-style." And biographer Jean Gould: Amy was "a female Henry VIII," she had "the soul of a sylph but the body of a hippopotamus." "Hippopoetess," Pound said (Witter Bynner, in another version): cruel for its being lopsidedly true. "Squat," "swollen," "stunted," "barrel-chested"…this chapter of her life is little more than a thesaurus for her bulk.

It shows most painfully in the diary she began to keep in 1889. She's fifteen, self-tormented, disclosing to its pages "I am ugly, fat, conspicuous, and dull. Oh Lord please let it be all right, and let Paul H. love me, and don't let me be a fool." But "Paul H." didn't love her. None of them loved her; the world was full of swan-necked debs. "I don't think that being all alone, in here, is good for me." And "I am doomed, for how can it be different— to see the man I love marry somebody else." And "I am doomed to be a dreadful pill; doomed to visibly blush, and waste my sweetness in the vicinity of the wall." And "I was a fool— *as usual!* a great rough masculine thing! But Paul! Oh! Good-night!"

The entry for January 13, 1889: "What would I not give to be a poet. Well day-dreams are day-dreams, & I never shall be…"

～

"And nightly," says the very chunky study of her by S. Foster

Damon, "she recorded faithfully the phase of the moon."

Whatever darkness ran through her life was somewhat alleviated by this lifelong, literal lunacy.

A full-plate moon with a garnish of cloud…

A camembert's rind…

A cameo…

Many nights it must have been the closest face she knew.

∼

Her best friends in her childhood were her books, and "dearest of all" was the one called *Moon-folk*. Here, "a lonely little girl makes the acquaintance of a chimney-elf"—and under his guidance, Rhoda drifts in a dory away to sea, then to the moon, where "all the persons of child literature, even to King Arthur and his knights," declare her welcome. It's easy to see why this was antidotal.

From then, the moon is a benign and serial punctuation. In California "I woke up in the night and the moon was beautiful." In Venice "We are having a moon, the very best moon that ever was, and we 'gondle' way out into the lagoon." In Egypt her boat, "a little dot of a thing only 75 ft. long"—a *dahabeah*—is named *Chonsu,* after the God of the rising moon, and "the moonlight on the Nile is more beautiful than any I have seen." It cuts its zags of liquid silver in the river chop, and each one for an instant is a chain, a badge, a ritual scimitar blade, for this devotee.

Its totemic presence lights her work from the first poem of her first book ("…the moon / Swings slow across the sky, / Athwart a waving pine…")—*athwart?*—to the posthumous Pulitzer-sanctioned collection ("A red moon leers beyond the lily-tank. A drunken moon ogling a sycamore, / Running long fingers down its shining flank…"). The poems are steeped in moon-brew. Quite likely, the poems would not have been written without the moon.

Because in 1891, when she was seventeen, and crying out with the ripeness of being seventeen, ajumble inside and neglected…the moon introduced her to someone.

⌒

> O Moon! old boughs lisp forth a holier din
> The while they feel thy airy fellowship.
> Thou dost bless every where, with silver lip
> Kissing dead things to life. The sleeping kine,
> Couch'd in thy brightness, dream of fields divine…

…and the "nested wren," and the "patient oyster"…everywhere, that utterly transforming, magesterial touch.

It's Keats, of course, in *Endymion*—a moonray is stirring his psychic quick into a rich Romantic lather. Douglas Bush reminds us "that poet and *persona* are one" in this poem, that "from his boyhood the moon had represented and consecrated all that Endymion loved and aspired to—nature, wisdom, poetry, friends, great deeds…"

She had a confidante now, a mentor. They shared the secret sign and handshake. She's walked out holding the moon in her eyes, this needy budding woman-child, and found a fellow cultist.

Jean Gould: "The effect of *Endymion* especially was like balm to her turbulent spirits. The erotic narrative clarified for her the relative values of the physical and spiritual in love and, fusing the two elements into one, showed her that both are essentially pure. The love scene in the second canto affected her for days: 'How many boys and girls have found solace and joy in this passage!' Her literary discoveries freed her from the prison of her body."

⌒

The format of her own first book was copied from that of Keats's

1820 volume *Lamia;* the title, *A Dome of Many-Coloured Glass,* is brazenly taken from Shelley's elegy for Keats; and two poems frankly conjure him—"He spurns life's human friendships to profess / Life's loneliness of dreaming ecstasy."

"I do not believe," she said, "that there is a person in the world who knows John Keats better than I do." Eventually she amassed the largest collection of Keatsiana in private hands, including the first edition of *Lamia* inscribed "F. B. from J. K.," Keats's presentation copy to Fanny Brawne, and—just as examples—the first drafts of "Eve of St. Agnes," "Ode to Autumn," and "On First Looking Into Chapman's Homer."

Damon claims that her monumental biography of Keats "took four years of her life and hastened her death." Overdramatic a statement or not, it's true that by then she was being broken apart by obesity, high blood pressure, hernia, sporadic gastritis, retina deterioration, and cardiac trouble. She finished the volume only after blood vessels burst in both of her eyes. Two volumes, actually: a total of 1,300 pages.

In her posthumous collection he's still with her, still the champion who healed her with his *Endymion:*

> Well John Keats,
> I know how you felt when you swung out of the inn
> And started up Box Hill after the moon.
> Lord! How she twinkled in and out of the box bushes
> Where they arched over the path.
> How she peeked at you and tempted you,
> And how you longed for the "naked waist" of her
> You had put into your secont canto.

Did he lay his fevered head against hers, although he'd been dead for seventy years, and the fluid moon poured back and forth between them, as if from one flask to another?

Yes, he lay his fevered head against hers, although he'd been dead for seventy years, and the fluid moon poured back and forth between them, as if from one flask to another.

～

Ask Louie, ask Rosie, they'll tell you: you can't talk moon, without dragging in the battered, baggage-filled heart.

～

After Egypt she visited Rome, to see the house in which Keats died, "and worshipped in true disciple form before its barred gateway." It's tempting, too, to leave her here—a white-robed keg-shaped pilgrim at the Temple of the Moon, performing her devotions.

But the anecdotes about this high-tone moxie-powered swaggerer of poetry are too, too good. My favorite occurs on the *Chonsu:* seventeen experienced, toughened Egyptian sailors are taking five supposedly helpless American women up the Nile. It's the job of the seasoned "cataract Arabs" to haul the *dahabeah* over the dangerous rapids. And this, with much rolling of eyes and imploring of extra bakhsheesh, they do—until the especially hazardous rapids near Philae, on the downriver return—and here they balk in a histrionic donkey-like show of recalcitrance. Let the squawky American she-sow empty her purse, if she wants this done! And what the American she-sow does?—she rolls her sleeves up, glowers fixedly at the *dahabeah* as if it's a bad dog needing a firm newspaper whack across the snout—and then she "stepped out and hoisted and hauled it to shore herself." Now *that's* Amy Lowell!

That, and the stogies. In a world in which the smoking of even cigarettes by the distaff sex was rigorously taboo (and, under

New York's "Sullivan Ordinance," illegal) Amy Lowell was famous for publicly and profusely puffing away on her trademark Manila cigars. When the threat of a World War also threatened to halt her regular supply of these, she ordered a special humidor built, something like the casket for a Pope, and stockpiled ten thousand at once.

Well, Abbott Lowell asks by way of logical ascertainment, what's the "big fat dame" of a lady driver doing at the moment?

"She's across the road here, sittin on a stone wall, smokin herself a cigar."

"In that case," President Lowell informs Mr. Rummle, "you may charge the bill. That is, I assure you, my sister."

~

In 1913 the "International Exhibition of Modern Art" will open at Armory Hall in New York—the "Armory Show"—and the staid, complacent surface of America's taste for realism will shirr and besquiggle and muckle itself in disturbing (and irrevocable) ways: Cubism, Post-Impressionism, Futurism, the fleshy glissando-like cylinder-glide of "Nude Descending a Staircase" by Duchamp, Brancusi's simplified fetish figures, Matisse's jazzy patterns… Slurs and lauds! Excitement and contumely! Nothing will be the same again.

And as a footnote to these artsy upheavals of 1913, Amy Lowell (and maid and limousine and chauffeur) will travel to London, there to take up residency in the posh top-floor retreat of the Berkeley Hotel (as always, masking her pangs with swank); and will visit (her singular purpose in being here) the tiny second-floor flat at 10 Church Walk, where the expatriate American Ezra Pound conducts his bohemian poetry masterminding.

He will already have heard of her coming: she has stormed herself into the offices of Constable's, the publishers, and demanded to know, in her brassiest manner, why she doesn't see copies of *A Dome of Many-Coloured Glass* in the bookstores here. She thinks she will remain in the publisher's offices until the books are found, unpacked, and distributed, thank you very much.

And she, of course, will have heard of this thorny spade-faced American maestro of "the new poetry," who had almost single-handedly invented (and is frenetically busy proselytizing) Imagism, who one night read a sestina for the "Poet's Club" at a restaurant in Soho "whereupon," said Glenn Hughes, "the entire café trembled." She will want the secrets to Imagism; will suffer his wheedling funds from her, and his cant. He will prune her writing of those *athwarts,* he will chill it clean with a dose of the hard no-nonsense brook-ice of his credo. She will read a new poem of hers at a dinner party, and at its most aqueous moment ("Splashing down moss-tarnished steps / It falls, the water; / And the air is throbbing with it…") he will enter the room with a miniature tin bathing tub for a helmet over his head. She will call him "thin-skinned." He will say "Aw shucks!" and brand her poetry "putrid." They will flatter and snipe and fortify their respective sides of what Heymann slyly calls "the ongoing skirmishes of the great poetry war."

Meanwhile, the other world, with its butcher saws and tribunals, continues its spin. The Archduke of Austria is assassinated. Austria-Hungary issues its forty-eight-hour ultimatum to Siberia, and five days later declares war. In a few days more, Great Britain follows.

Amy Lowell will see it all take place: "A great crowd of people with flags marched down Piccadilly, shouting 'We want war! We want war!' They sang the Marseillaise, and it sounded savage, abominable. The blood lust was coming back, which we had hoped was gone forever from civilized races." It turns out, the worlds of our little day-to-day love and competitiveness are gerbil-wheels in larger wheels, in infrastructure of cosmologic proportion, not Ptolemy, Einstein, or Hawking can wholly cartograph.

She will come to know and befriend the British poet Rupert Brooke ("perhaps the most notable British poet of his time"). She will attend his reading at London's Poetry Bookshop ("Louder! Louder!" she calls, at his indistinct delivery). Two months later he'll be dead in the trenches in France.

~

But that's all in the future, though the immediate future. Right now it's 1912. Robert Frost is sprawled on the floor of his temporary home in rural England, winnowing poems from the raggedy sheaf of poems that will be his first book. Robinson Jeffers, Vachel Lindsay, Joyce Kilmer, Elinor Wylie, Ezra Pound, and Edna St. Vincent Millay, are first breaking into print.

In Paris, Picasso and Braque are busy upping the ante in a private back-and-forth in which they're making the very small but revolutionary step of incorporating printed commercial lettering and design (for instance, cut-up newspaper headlines) into their paintings: Picasso's *Table with Bottle, Wineglass and Newspaper* (each of the first three drawn, and the fourth a pasted patch of actual front-page newspaper). Gopnik and Varnedoe say "the private innovations of Braque and Picasso's little conversation in 1912 became, by a few intermediary steps and within a decade, a signal part of the official public language of a nation."

And, in Chicago, Miss Harriet Monroe is piecing together the initial issue of *Poetry: A Magazine of Verse,* that will appear September 1912. Ezra Pound is on the masthead as "foreign editor." Eliot, Williams, Hilda Dolittle, Stevens will soon appear in its pages. Amy Lowell receives a solicitation of money and poems.

A Dome of Many-Coloured Glass is published in 1912. Its first year out, it sells just eighty copies. Louis Untermeyer, writing in the *Chicago Evening Post,* says that the book "to be brief, in spite of its lifeless classicism, can never rouse one's anger. But, to be briefer still, it cannot rouse one at all." That year, the textile workers of Lawrence and Lowell stage a record-breaking two-month strike. The Lowells are painted as money-minded, whip-wielding robber barons. The State Police kill two mill workers in cold blood. Everything's shattering, each day is a rare plate thrown at the wall. She locks herself in her third-floor bedroom, hugging her walrusy self, ashamed that she's weeping—but weeping. It's midnight and she stares at the sky with the emptied-out face of a wax museum statue. Gloom and griping: barrel-chested Amy going over the falls…

But she knows someone who—guaranteed—will rejuvenate her, someone she hasn't seen for years, and never in his own far headquarters; someone who can rub away this recent sickly moss. She sends a telegram: HAIL MARSOLEUM STOP EXPECT YOUR SCRIVENER SIBLING SATURDAY 3 PM TRAIN STOP IN NEED OF A FAMILY FROLIC STOP WILL TRADE YOUR STANZAS FOR STARS STOP POSTSCRIPT.

Maybe he'll even show her her moon.

~

But Percival Lowell isn't sure that any of his guests arriving later this afternoon will be able to see so much as a hardboiled egg held three feet away from The Master Unit's unresponsive eye. He stares at Slipher and Slipher and Lampland, there in his study, from the middle of a mood that's slumping quickly into despondency. Then, from the observatory, they hear a tinny shriek.

Tolliver rushes in: "It's working!" They gape at him in disbelief.

"Mr. Tolliver..." he's almost afraid to ask it directly "...am I to understand that you have repaired The Master Unit?"

"Yes sir! Well, no. *I* didn't repair it," and now some hesitancy stipples poor Tolliver's uniform rush of pleasure, "but *some-body...*" Tolliver looks from Slipher to Slipher to Lampland; none of the three responds. "Well, *somebody* shimmed it, sir, and now it's working, I tell you!"

"*Shimmed* it, Mr. Tolliver?"—as if he might be saying in public *masturbated* or *butt-fucked.*

"Uh, yes sir. Shimmed it. You know, sir: like when you set a chip of wood or a matches box beneath the uneven leg of a..."

"Yes, Mr. Tolliver. I understand the concept. Gentlemen," waving his hand like a gracious host on a house tour, "let us see."

Yes, there's the observatory. There, in its center, probing toward the heavens like an altar unto the gods, is The Master Unit. And under one of its dainty, exquisite legs is the current issue of *All-Story.*

"Under the Moons of Mars!" the cover blurts. June 1912.

"Mr. Tolliver."

"Yes sir?"

"*Would* you be so good as to bring the custodian's assistant in here?"

4.

"At once, upon hearing the blood-chilling scream of a female voice in that haunted scene, I commenced to bound across the crimson sward of those dead sea-bottoms with the giant leaps allowed my Earthly muscles by the weaker Barsoomian gravity. At the first, my longsword was in my hand, prepared for any contingency, no matter how savage, for mingled with those piteous screams I had heard the exultant, throaty growl of the great white ape of Barsoom.

"The growls continued as I neared the toppled, overgrown columns and crumbling public walls of the ruin of one of those long-ago abandoned port cities that sporadically dot these wastes. The woman's screams, however, had ceased, and I feared that, even now, I might be too late to free her from the fate that awaits the luckless Barsoomian maiden who falls prey to these beasts. The thought that she might be, was almost surely, my beloved, increased both the fear and the urgency of my mad dash.

"The two moons, Cluros and Thuria, leant their eerie double shadows to the night. When at last I had frantically searched through what seemed to me to be half of the caved-in buildings of that formerly glorious city, I came upon my objective. The great white ape was towering above the curled-up form of a woman whose sheer, ripped silks revealed a body bruised and scratched, but quivering yet with life. Her face was turned from me, but who she was, and how she came to be here, were questions that needed their asking delayed, for now I confronted this interrupted, thus doubly-enraged, representative of the most feared of the dead-sea-bottom creatures.

"The great white ape stands ten feet tall, hairless except for a shock of bristly fur upon its head. Its snout and teeth are not unlike the Earth gorilla's, although millennia of cruelty have given these an especially devilish aspect. An intermediary set of arms is located midway between its upper and lower limbs—altogether, a very unpleasant opponent. This one carried a cudgel, and no sooner had I entered the vast ruined hallway where it had dragged its prey, than its club and my sword were adversaries swirling through the night for blood.

"The details of that battle I cannot recall, so swiftly and confusingly did they take place. I know I was wounded once on the shoulder, and I know I gave back more than I received. When it was over, and that giant body lay damp and still at my feet, I leaped to the corner, and kneeled worriedly at the side of the terror-struck woman, and then turned her face to the moons' light.

"'Louie Louie Louie. Vhy do you think soch thinks?'

"'Rosie?'

"'Yah, of course, *Rosie*. Who else? A Princess from outer spaces maybe?'

"'Oh no, no… But—kvick, before more of the apes return, I must rescue you!'

"'Louie. Look around, Louie. *You're* the vun needs the rescue. Yah?'"

~

My grandfather milked the cow. Her name was Venus, a patchy thing of white with licorice spotting. He liked her fleshy good looks, she had Poland written all over her. Satellite, the calf, explored the fenced-in demi-pasture in woozy figure eights.

The milking shed was cool. On days when the sun was like a red injection of army ants under his skin, he'd come to the grayly lavender shade of the shed, and press the dented tin of the empty pail against his forehead.

He'd hum. He'd squeeze the ivory withes of milk from her udder, and pretend it was a bagpipes of a sort, and he'd hum some popular tune he'd picked up in town, "The Inky-Tink Song" or "A Soldier's Light" or "Gay Plantation Slippers," or sometimes a Polish children's counting-rhyme, "Chicken-Cabbage-Chicken." But the love songs, either *au courant* or folkloric, he refrained from humming. He didn't want to think about love.

And even so, he daydreamed. Sometimes her face was so tightly pressed against his own, and he was so open to this, that when something startled him out of that world, he thought he'd find himself impressed like dough or wet clay. And occasionally—not often, but occasionally—a female guest stayed overnight at the Main House: men are men, after all, he reasoned, even if they *do* devote themselves to something so fantastically diddleheaded as counting the stars.

He was too polite and (let's face it) unwanted, to sidle up to these slim, pastel, frilled visitors for a drinking-in of their otherness. But he'd see them from the toolshed or the pasture as they breakfasted on the piazza. Then, the usual hobnailed sentences that stomped through the air of Mars Hill—"Oh dammit, Lampland, I told you the arc declined by seven degrees!"—became the silkier, trilled communiqués of "Do you *haaave* to get back to those silly charts?" (the eyelashes almost audibly batting around the words, like a flock of birds) or "Honey, you can stop looking—I found the hat pins!"

Hot pants, my grandfather heard.

∿

O sovereign power of love! O grief! O balm!
All records, saving thine, come cool, and calm,
And shadowy, through the mist of passed years:
For others, good or bad, hatred and tears
Have become indolent; but touching thine,
One sigh doth echo, one poor sob doth pine...
Etc. etc. etc. Ask Louie. Ask Keats,

Who looks back to his page now and completes
These lines from *Endymion* (that I quote above
To demonstrate the brotherhood of love).

∿

His room in what they called "the netherworld" of the enclave was small and spare, but fit his purposes. By its very plainness, it was like blank canvas; every day, in his mind, he tried to paint a believable future across it.

Every evening, when the work was done and the last free-floating smatter of the mesa's sun was snuffled by dusk, he untied the satchel in which he kept a "barbershop magazine": its cover featured a famous New York dancehall girl in a waspwaist corset, her stockings were unrolled to the knee. He lit a cigarette, and leaned lazily back. His smoke became the smoky air of the hall in which she performed…

And every morning he lifted out, from beneath his pillow, the pamphlet of *shachris, mincha* and *mahriv* prayers. You could barely say it still existed: he could hold it to the morning light and see his fingers through it, like fish in turbid water. But the Word of God had been poured forth from shakier vessels than this. It served its secular purpose too: as once it connected him back to Mother Poland, now it kept him tied to those earliest days on the Lower East Side, when the skin of his skin was goosefleshed alive every second with misery, burning hopes, and lovetussle over a floor of chicken feathers…

It didn't matter, the barbershop girl or the Holy Word Itself, he came to see it all led back to this Rosie. More and more, want to or not, her face was painted, in his mind, over the blank walls of Arizona.

～

Smuddle was his immediate supervisor; Smuddle was "groundskeeper," he reported to Meacham, "observatory assistant." Meacham reported to C. V. Tolliver. The men liked Louie, he was "okay." A little too foreign, yes, and he kept to himself. But he could take a joke. His accent alone was a rootietoot hoot that could lilt the most boring of conversations. And he could fix anything—*anything*. Smuddle told Meacham, and Meacham told Tolliver, how this Louis fellow had never *been* behind an automotorcar's wheel before, but Smuddle unfolded the Dracula's-cape-like hood of his dormant machine and this what's-his-name, Louis, intuitively knew, he *knew,* and fifteen minutes later it was running again. So I gave him a package of cigarettes.

What Louie thought of *them?* In a way, they were lesser gods serving The Great God Lowell. Louie would daily see him in the Mars Hill garden, tending with a paternal air to his justly-famous, robust squashes and pumpkins (Louie wasn't allowed in the garden, but would keep its row of tools in clean, tight, regimental readiness). Taxis swooped down for these people like golden chariots out of clouds. Photographers begged for admission. They seemed to live in some ever-scintillating effluvium, spangled with planets and stars. They made The-Man-Who-Owned-All-Of-Forman-Street look like a shoeshine boy by contrast.

And yet, they were children. They laughed at such simple things, they bickered like boys in gymnasium choosing up teams. They could use the 2-gauge tightening swivel, then set it down, and it would be lost for hours ("Slipher, have *you* seen…?"). They lived in dreams, their heads would disappear in the sky for days on end, like creatures out of fable, or like five-year-olds under the tablecloth, in a magic domain, thinking nobody else can see them. My grandfather knew, *Der kholmer iz a nar*, The dreamer's a fool. He shook his own head, he *tsked* at them fondly.

Meacham offered him cigarettes. Mostly, he was ignored. They gave him little more heed than he gave the turquoise gyroscope of flies around Venus's rump. He wandered, benign himself and unmolested in turn, past windows, through offices, around the Black Forest of dials and wires that fed the observatory, he watched them cater like priests to the needs of The Master Unit. Tolliver told him a joke once, a woman and a bear. Once,

Meacham tried to initiate him into the orthodoxies of poker. And Smuddle taught him to drive.

Each week he made the trip into town, with their list of miscellaneous items. And he would check the rack at Larcher's Necessaries! & Quiddities! for the latest *All-Story*. He couldn't get enough of John Carter's splendid deed-filled adventures on Mars.

~

It was published as "Under the Moons of Mars" in six install-ments, starting in February 1912 (retitled *A Princess of Mars* for the book, in 1917). He signed his opus "Normal Bean"—to tell the world, this flimsy escapism came from someone "normal in the head." (*All-Story* understandably read the written signature as "Norman Bean," and this became the byline.) Fifty-two years after, the series was still being gobbled by an avid worldwide readership (*John Carter of Mars*, the eleventh book, was published by Canaveral Press in 1964) and, through its imitators, had virtually defined a science-fantasy subgenre.

An enlistee in the Seventh Cavalry, Burroughs had spent two bleak years in the Arizona Territory (1895-97: the formative Mars-espying years of the Lowell Observatory). Surely this accounts, in part, for the heartfelt (though repetitive) portrayal of the desert in his framing-story, that sets us up for John Carter's being spirited to Mars.

"Few western wonders are more inspiring than the beauties of an Arizona moonlit landscape; the silvered mountains in the distance, the details of the stiff, yet beautiful cacti form a picture at once enchanting and inspiring…"

But—Arizona; and then a protagonist mystically whisked to a Mars striated by engineered canals? It can't be Burroughs's early cavalry days are enough to account for his choice of these two em-phatically-rendered locations. John Flint Roy: "That Burroughs read and made use of Percival Lowell's books *Mars and Its Canals* and *Mars as the Abode of Life* cannot be denied."

"...My attention was quickly riveted by a large red star close to the distant horizon. As I gazed upon it I felt a spell of over-powering fascination. It seemed to call me across the unthink-able void, to lure me to it, to draw me as the lodestone attracts a particle of iron..."

Green men. White apes. Red dunes. It begins.

~

And Arizona, to Louie? He had hours to fill as he pleased, too in-significant a worker to be timeclocked. Often, to or from his erranding at Larcher's, he would drive the Smuddlemobile along a desert maze spun out of his own spontaneous concocting.

Prodigious gunnysacks of color seemed to open on the mesa tops, and scrolls of it—salsa reds and vivid bunting blues and oolitic earthtones lifted straight from the fundament—unrolled down the seamed, deep-sienna sides.

He watched a lady's beaded bag, a glinting polyp of jet and crimson, suddenly spring and land vigilant: a desert lizard. Some were ruffed, like Elizabethan courtiers. He'd seen them mating. The male had two penises, both barbed. Their eyes are tight black berries, staring out of folds of ancient saurian granulation.

A roadrunner sprinted across the track, a limp snake pinched in its beak. A jackrabbit halted, as still as if it were painted on an old-time tavern sign. Its ears were huge highstanding floral-look-ing sculls—so thin that, backed as they were by the morning sun, my grandfather clearly saw their filamental networks of blood vessels, ruby on light buff (desert-functional: the air in breezing past them cools the blood).

The creosote bush will grow continuously for 12,000 years—the oldest known living organism. It spreads out from its center, the stems on the inside dying, the stems on the outside ever-pioneering—this can eventually make a green ring up to twenty-five feet in diameter, on the sands. My grandfather stopped the car. There was nobody, only the buffs and the duns and the ambers, and the durable mother-of-all-blues in the sky. There was nobody, only my grandfather. He was the demiurge here, the djinn, he skipped to the center of the circle and whooped, he twirled in place, a feral, energy-spewing creature, spinning to keep the universe on its axis.

Monstrous, wonder-ridden: it may as well have been Barsoom.

"Good." One afternoon at Larcher's he counted out ten cents to an impassive-faced Native American customer shuffling there short by exactly a dime. The Indian's uncracked stoniness was—dignity? anger? My grandfather couldn't tell. "Good" was his only response, then the purchase was made, and the man was gone in a stride. Another white might not have been the recipient even of that single word. But my grandfather gave out the wavelengths of a fellow alien wandering here amid the rows of garden hoses and after-dinner mints.

A world was coming undone by 1912, you could have watched it happen from the vantage of the Larcher's cash register. Recipes for cholla buds, palo verde beans, amaranth greens, the pads of the prickly pear, incendiary mescal, were being replaced by canned and, later, refrigerated grocery goods. This supplantation will increase by the New Deal 1930's (the ethnobotany diet, gone to Cokes and burger patties) with diabetes, hypertension, and chronic obesity its legacy. The principle is Newtonian in lucidity: two worlds cannot equally occupy one point.

Of course my grandfather wouldn't have known this, any more than the Larcher's cashier or the Indian customer or the well-intended federal food-welfare corpsmen knew it.

But he did know—after all, he was born in a culture where *dybbuks* scrammed from behind the grain trough when you lit a candle—he knew that when he drove through the desert at twilight, spirits skirled in the air, they left their *kachinas* like genies freed for the night from their lamps, they populated the gusts and the thermals and brushed his cheek indifferently, as if to say he wasn't of their tribe, their kind, but neither was he lost beyond the edge of their recognition.

Are these gods? or are these cycles of moisture-exchange in an arid system? He drove, he followed a line of radio-wail and blood-pull that preceded Ur of the Chaldees on this Earth.

It stripped his skin off like old wallpaper. It was magma and thump and theophany in his heart.

And the moon, its bag of bonelight tangled over the mountains.

~

The Arizona moon floats over Krazy's Coconino with such frequency, it's almost a regular citizen of the cast—sometimes as thin as a sickle of cellophane; at others, as rounded and solid as a yellow carnival bump-'em car.

The Navajo night chant, the "Yeibichai," goes:

> *With beauty may I walk.*
> *With beauty before me, may I walk.*
> *With beauty behind me, may I walk.*
> *With beauty above me, may I walk.*
> *With beauty below me, may I walk.*
> *With beauty all around me, may I walk.*

And Officer Pupp soliloquizes:

Today my world walks in beauty.
Beneath me a good earth—
A gracious glebe, lies in beauty—
Shifting sands dust its cheeks in powdered beauty—
And now will I turn my eye to the empyrean—
Where stars' gleam moon's beam

…

So—I'll nap in beauty.

Dat debbil moon. Oh lair of chaste splendor!

~

Varnedoe and Gopnick suggest that "the squiggled needle and monoliths" and similar vertical structures in the oil paintings of Joan Miro (in illustration of which they reproduce his 1926 painting *Dog Barking at the Moon*, with its ladder reaching from the ground-plane to the sky) have correspondence with "Herriman's great stone fingers"—those monumental, sometimes spire-like lithic formations of the Arizona deserts, that he captured in his own mad manner. "Both devices suggest an enchanted universe where heaven and earth still adjoin, like tenement apartments connected by a fire escape."

Herriman's father "operated a barbershop, owned a bakery, and dabbled in astronomy." So it isn't surprising the son grows up to know how our lathers and doughs can rise alongside our sidereal aspirations.

One Sunday, Ignatz rigs a half-price (lensless) telescope for Krazy, and lifts a flimflam crescent moon on a wire (it looks something like a croissant): "I see a moons, a marvillis moons," she oohs.

But what Herriman also knows is how the "marvillis" is shaped by the "beholda's" eye. Another Sunday, Pupp says to

Krazy, "Nice circle around (the) l'il old moon tonight, eh, 'K.'?"
"Soikol?" she asks, and looks to see an impressive triangle
framing the moon. "Yes—circle."

"He mins a 'try-ankle," Krazy explains to Ignatz. So now *he*
looks…there's the moon, inside a luminous square.

In one panel, it will be rubicond; the next, as green as sweet
chilies. Here, as wheezed-out as a flat tire; there, as plump as a
bratwurst bursting out of its own rich blotchy casing. Orchida-
ceously lush or as matter-of-fact as a subway token, it swoops the
cockamamie Coconino overspaces in whatever guise is necessary,
a small disquisition on *relativism*, in lunar "lengwidge" as trans-
lated by George Herriman: it's a squib of toothpaste or paint
from the tube, a penny squooshed on the railroad tracks, a proto-
zoan paisley of Picasso-like conjecture far ahead of its time, a
gorgeous thumb-printed pretzel-twist of a moon that could
have been baked in a kiln, molybdenum, spongey, amuletic,
pingpongesque, whatever.

> Say a man looks at the moon.
> A woman looks at the moon.
> That makes two moons.

~

It was silver tonight, so painfully, *sharply* exquisite…Keats
needed to turn from the cottage's window. He was reminded of
the cutting tools he'd seen them use when he was an apprentice
in the surgery wards. He felt the moon could enter him that way
tonight. "And I've *already* lost my heart," he said.

He was waiting for her, she promised she'd manage to get away
from her own enormous gauntlet of household duties by eight—
it must have been half-past now, at least. He shuffled a sheaf of

pages from *Endymion*, impatiently. "O Moon! far-spooming Ocean bows to thee…" and shuffled again:

> …Despair! despair!
> He saw her body fading gaunt and spare
> In the cold moonshine. Straight he seiz'd her wrist;
> It melted from his grasp: her hand he kiss'd,
> And, horror! kiss'd his own—he was alone.

—too true. It must be nearing on nine. And then he thought he heard—he did hear, footsteps, skipping up the rush-strewn gravel path! The heart he claimed he'd lost was doing wild calisthenics in his throat. There was a bashful knock, he hurried to the door and flung it open—

"*Amy?*"

"Well, John," *(puff)* "who" *(puff)* "were you expecting?"

"Amy, please: you know those vile things exacerbate my coughing."

~

She woke and found herself chuckling, and had the wisdom to carry her dream-chuckle into a hearty, wakeful laugh. Keats, still!—canoodling about in her brain-muck all these years! When she returned to Boston she'd be sure to tell Ada of this, and then they'd both chuckle, lightly holding one another in the ring of sixteen pillows.

Ah, but Ada was many hundreds of miles away now, and the maid, and the maroon platoon of drivers. *This* trip, her first this way, was solo. Somehow it needed to be. She closed her eyes, she imagined the ties of the railroad tracks at such speed, that they blended into a single length of excellent parquet-work, the kind in her second-floor study.

She shifted her aching kielbasa body in its seat. A first class seat!—it could have been a crate for oranges! And some of these other "first-class" passengers!—there was a woman, *foreign*, smelled it, talked it (guttural rollings), dressed it with her three rough-woven scarves worn simultaneously, an *anarchist*. In the darkness, in the aloneness, Amy was sure of it. An anarchist, with an oilcloth bag that might have held bombs. She gave off a mixture of cheap cologne and garlic.

When the porter announced that Providence, the marvels of twentieth-century technology, and seven optional small-town stops that the newlywed engineer had simply ignored in his passion to turn back East, meant they would arrive three hours ahead of schedule, Amy gleamed with relief.

She stared out the window and watched the moon make sterling silver service of the trees. Next stop, Arizona.

~

"Louis? I merely request an explanation."

Some nights, with a bottle of sugary wine from Larcher's never-failing provender in his pocket, and soon in his blood, my grandfather found himself leaning fraternally (if cautiously) against a great saguaro in the nearby desert, telling it his problems, or singing softly to it, or simply trying to hear the slow green thrum of its own deep-pitched interior life. And this saguaro was as familiar to him as, say, a Hassidic Jew—that is, extreme; but knowable.

Here, though, with the eyes of the pantheon Tolliver, Slipher, Slipher, Lampland and Lowell upon him, Louie knew that he faced an alien consciousness. "Vahsheenktun, Jafferson, Vahsheenktun," he incanted under his breath. It was all that could come to him in his time of need, an American lucky mantra. Then Tolliver caught his eye. He'd spoken a few times to Tolliver. If he tried, now, to remind this man of their earlier camaraderie...? "Misters. A voman, she meets the bear in the voods. The bear says..."

"Louie: no. Sir," he turned to Lowell, "I've conversed with the man, a little. I believe... Sir?" Lowell was holding *All-Story*, flipping through its pulp pages. Semi-naked Martian paramours, Martian swordsmen... He threw it out the door, into the antechamber, an energetic overhand pitch; for added effect, he walked to the door and carefully, coolly closed it.

"I'm sorry, Mr. Tolliver. You were saying?"

"That I believe this man, who has demonstrated intuitive abilities with mechanical problems, may have...may have knowingly... What I mean is, he may have helped us..."

"There is no denying, Mr. Tolliver, that this Louis has helped us." They continued to talk as if he were rooms away. "I should like to determine how accidentally, or how intentionally. And I should like to establish, for this Louis's sake and our own peace of mind, some sets of clearer guidelines for access by the unauthorized to the observatory."

This went on for quite some while. At one point Lowell said to Louie, as if not sure if he were addressing an *idiot savante* or a captured circus ape, "The stars, Louis." Indicating *up* with his forefinger. "What do you know about the stars?"

"Vell, vhen they fall—this means God is closer to the world. Then God is lissning to us."

Lowell stared. The staff had never seen Old Ironballs stare this way. He still couldn't tell if he was dealing with pawky ingenuity or idiocy.

But the story of how my grandfather halted the great man in his inquisition, has come down to the family, mixed, eventually, with a version of Einstein's saying he couldn't believe that God played dice with the universe. "See?" someone would say, Aunt

Tillie or maybe one of the Pinkuses. "See? *mitt* the stars, *mitt* Gott. He knew, I tell you, chust like Einstein, a *cheenyus!*"

⁓

Here, I need to remember that Lowell reads popular detective stories; *The Maulevener Murders,* for instance, is on his shelves. He has his circumlocutious wit. He isn't the worst stuffed shirt the Boston gentry has produced.

But these are tender times. The surer he is of his melt-conducting canals, the more his theories are mocked. And now this—this *bumwipe* of a magazine! And this savvily nitwit floorsweeper! He's exasperated, tired suddenly down to his body's bottommost cobblestone byways. All he can do is stare, and that's how Meacham finds them when he coughs by way of self-announcement and peeks in from the antechamber.

"Sir? Mr. Lowell?"—he's whispering.

Tolliver answers on behalf of his chief. "What, Meacham?"

An orotund stage whisper now: "Them newspaper fellas are—"

Here. With their being a little early, and Louie's draconian questioning running so long… The minions of Mars Hill all are staring as wide-eyed as Lowell now. A beaming, beefy man in a species of derby gives a shake and push to Meacham's hand, as if it were a latch, and Meacham a door; and Meacham, in fact, can't help but act the part, he seems to swivel open. A knot of four of Hearst's reporters enters the room.

"Mr. Lowell! Sorry to barge in early but, well, what good are canals without barges?" Derby barks appreciatively at his own joke. Lowell pales. The other three mean nothing to him, but Derby—! Derby is Garrett P. Serviss, skeptic, and captain of science-column writers for the Hearst chain. It takes only a second for Lowell to see this, to understand the importance of creating a pristinely strong impression, and to realize that the ridiculous situation with this shabby janitorial type now center-stage requires expeditious, subtle maneuvering.

In this same second, Lowell's élan returns. He'll merely dismiss the intrusive Louis for now, and swiftly move to rounds of champagne while Tolliver ably manages to re-shim The Master Unit with something more seemly, perhaps a lacquered cedarwood plaque from the study, perhaps…

But this is a busy second. One of the other reporters, a rumpled sort in a lumpish Stetson hat, has set his bristol board down on the floor, and is dashing excitedly, arms open, to the center of the room, as if greeting a relative at a railway station, but that can't be.

"Lou-boy!" and he's hugging the under-custodian. "Lou-boy, you tickle my buzzum!" He claps him roughly on the shoulders.

"My bosom is also funny from you, mine friend."

"And a lady," Serviss says, with a courtly doffing of his derby, "who accompanied us from town in our taxi."

"Louie!"

"Rosie!" And she drops her bulging oilcloth bag with a thump.

The Master Unit, gentlemen, serves not only Mars Hill but the scientific community on an international scale, as you can see by a small demonstration my staff and I have dribbles away like so much running tapioca pudding, good-bye, it was nice while it lasted, farewell to thee, oh golden one.

Now *everybody's* staring—Lowell, the Lowell subalterns, Hearst's quartet—at Louie, who has some explaining to do.

He points to Rosie.

"Mine luff," he explains.

Herriman grins like a proud proud papa. "Percival, doesn't this call for champagne?"

⌒

"Hell (pardon me, ma'am) but any friend of George's" and Garrett P. Serviss gestures expansively toward the Stetson-hatted grinner, "is a friend of mine and a friend of William Randolph Hearst himself, I'll wager, and so is his friend's true lady-love!"

And so Percival Lowell finds himself ringing for Meacham and, by God, five minutes later champagne indeed is flowing co-piously, and toasts go around to the reunited couple, who stand there dazed and fitfully whispering phlegmy, gravelly foreign sentiments to each other.

Anyway, *Louie* is dazed. He and Lowell have this, at least, in common. Their stares around the room-at-large resemble the look of mounted deer heads. If anybody here is assured and at ease, it's the foreignest one in the room. But Rosie is happily doing what she'd come to do—reclaiming her man—and doing it quicker, it seems, and in loftier style than she'd ever imagined when the wives of Louie's friends chipped in for her own "first-cless" train ticket to Flagstaff. New in the state by an hour and in the *sanctum sanctorum* observatory by only five minutes, she stands near Louie nodding at the rounds of lifted glasses with regal comportment, as if she were used to the gathered masses bestowing her compliments. The Master Unit backdrops her as if it were constructed with this single purpose in mind: to be the intricate, yea, museum-quality frame around Rosie-from-Cowflop-Poland, Rosie-Come-to-America, for whom the stars and the planets have now been made to stop in their tracks.

My grandmother Rosie, the Queen of the Universe.

And all this while, Lowell—with looks of vague imploration to Tolliver—is hoping their social boil will simmer down, after all it's still possible, and some *soupçon* of factual Martian newsworthi-ness be broached.

By "all this while" I mean—what? thirty minutes? Enough for the other taxi to finally wind its way to Mars Hill. And it would have been sooner, but first her thirteen suitcases needed gathering up—more than the luggage department at the Flagstaff depot has handled so far all month.

She sees the front door is ajar; Meacham is nowhere about. She spends ten minutes browsing a magazine she finds, *All-Story;* and then, not really caring who she interrupts or why, she opens the observatory door, she peers commandingly over the screwy cocktail scene with consummate Amy Lowell hauteur.

They turn to face a heap of ghee grandstyled in formal diamonded black. "No wonder you see those lines all over Mars, Percy. Offer me a drink and I'll see them with you." She gives them a smile that's won (or at least intimidated) the hearts of kings and philosophers.

And Lowell, stunned by her sudden apperarance (he'd planned on having Smuddle meet her at the train at 3 P.M.) but also delighted—his sister, his little sister! *someone who will understand!*—Lowell seamlessly meets the occasion. "Gentlemen: Miss! Amy! Lowell!" and this is what does it: "the Poet." She radiates.

Then he politely corrects himself. "Gentlemen *and* lady," nodding toward Rosie.

Who Amy notices now. "Percy! That woman, her bag—! She has BOMBS!"

It happened this way. It happened in the Barsoomian dimension. I call it "the Syzygy of 1912."

5.

That year, the Arizona Territory becomes the state of Arizona. Chagall completes *The Cattle Dealer.* The S.S. Titanic sinks: 1,513 drown. The process for manufacturing cellophane is invented by Edwin Brandenberger. Victor F. Hess discovers cosmic radiation. The shaped remains of that charlatan ancestor, Piltdown Man, are found near Lewes (and won't be proved a hoax for forty-one years more). Ravel's ballet of "Daphnis and Chloe" opens in Paris. Carl Jung's *The Theory of Psychoanalysis* appears, as does the new word "vitamin" (coined by the chemist Kasimir Funk).

And Picasso is dabbing away at *The Scallop Shell*, his oil-and-enamel-on-canvas that uses (and so coopts?) a faithful image of the cover of *Notre Avenir est dans l'air,* a 1912 brochure exhorting France to develop aeronautics for military power. Contrapuntal, squinting-artist-yin and goggled-fighter-pilot-yang, these two zoom into the binary world, here a world, there a world, everywhere a whirled world... It might be as unthinkably large as global war... It might be Wilson's cloud-chamber photographs done in 1912 that lead, at last, to the detection of electrons and protons...

"Kiss my ass," says Larcher to the shipment driver unloading his cases of syrup. This Coca-Cola drink is five cents a glass, as much as a three-egg breakfast with grits, but the thirsty minions of Flagstaff, Arizona can't get enough of it! And here's this dinkass delivery man who thinks he can drop off *half* a shipment, and credit the store toward shipment-and-a-half *next* month! *Suuure.* What a world!

~

...That's all so far, or seemingly far, away.

The brouhaha's ha'd-out. Elliptic explanations have been offered and accepted; and we find them now, ten men, two women, tentatively stitched together around a common appreciation of Percival Lowell's champagne and Rosie Kaplan's loaves of braided egg-glaze *challah,* that an hour ago were unwrapped from their waxy swaddle in proof that they were balms of a sort, not bombs. They go especially well with the jars of pickled herring she'd brought, and the capers and chutney Lowell directs be excavated from miscellania-level in the pantry.

"EX-cellent bakery goods!" says Slipher the elder a third time, diving into the rick of herrings on his plate, then sandwiching one in a folded *challah* slice. "Still fresh, despite the train ride! You know, Miss Kaplan," and here he brandishes his fork in the air like Liberty her torch, "our friends at Larcher's in the city—Louis, do you know Larcher's?—stock a bread inferior to this as, say, the catfish is to the salmon. If you were to share the secrets behind this with our friends there—for remuneration, of course—I believe the entire Flagstaff community would be in your debt."

A general huzzah of assent from everybody breaks forth, although Louie is half-devoted to studying Rosie's ankles where they're delicately paired beneath her hem; and Lowell is busy with two thin metal rods he's slid from the core of The Master Unit, with which he's demonstrating the employment of chopsticks to Garrett P. Serviss; and Herriman is in heaven, hat tilted back on his head, feet propped up on a pseudo-hassock improvised from Rosie's sturdy hat box, sketching, sketching!

"Let's see…," Tolliver tries. *"Auntie Rosie's Baked Goods!"* Then he looks at Amy and slips her a wink. *"An explosion of taste in each bite."*

∽

It's evening. He *won't* take "no" for an answer. His distinguished guests from the Hearst empire will stay the night in the Mars Hill baronial guest quarters. Just now, Lampland is beginning the demonstration of The Master Unit—deftly and persuasively, it should be said—having risen in rank to Explainer Supreme, so the sibling reunion can deepen (from its flurried, dramatic after-

∴ 158 ∴

noon start) in Lowell's study. Suddenly this is vastly more important to him than wooing the flunkies of Hearst or anyone else.

"Oh, Amy, what a vexatious day!"

"These are vexatious times." She's sitting, a living rotunda, on the dragonfoot mahogany sofa (upholstered in red, with fine black striping, it could almost be a design his dearly-defended canals have inspired). "Parlous, parlous times," she addends. They each have one of his Cuban cheroots in hand, and they each gaze into its rising writhe of smoke as if an oracle might spell the terms of the future there.

"And this *hell*damn Democrat Wilson who's in office now—! Amy, back East…"

"…are troubles, Percy. The mills are fomenting. The center of our lives, I'm afraid, is coming undone. I'm so scared sometimes, Percy. Not even Ada can coddle me out of it. And my book…" her defenses are down in this room, she doesn't need to be The Brass Valkyrie here "…what they've done to my book…" She turns her head, so he won't have to be ashamed for her visible weakness.

"Amy!" his lips purse out a raspberry of derision, "Hang the reviewers! Hang the public too! Hang 'em or buy 'em off, but don't let the dundernoggins stop you. Look, those men out there, from the newspaper—?" and his eyes switch from a lovely bronze-and-polished-rosewood orrery on his desk, to the study door. Does he hear a cabal, even now, tiptoeing up to the other side? "For eighteen years, off and on, again and again, this is what they've tried doing to me." He snaps his cheroot in half.

"Don't go and operatically pluck your nerves on my account, Percy. I'm sorry. You're tired, I can see it, don't fib. Your eyes are red."

"Yes. But it isn't anger or weariness, little Postscript. It's Mars. I swear the color's rubbed off on me, and in me, I probably *piss* red. Amy, I look, and I *look*, I know that planet better than most men know the skin of their wives, and no one believes me. Well, some do. My men here, Flammarion over in France, but... Amy, it isn't even my *sight* that goes up the telescope by now, but a connective tissue."

"Look..." he lifts a paperweight (it's Mars, the size of a softball) and flashes a handful of graphs in front of her. "Just from last month. Sightings of double canals, with atmospheric condition at the times of sighting noted. If you knew the moon this well..."

"Now, Percy; there are moons and there are *moons*. I think my darling moon" and here she rummages in her purse, then fishes out the much-crumpled *All-Story* (he's astonished, of course: is he cursed? won't this thing *ever* disappear?) "must be more like *this* Mars than yours." She sees his face. "Don't be disappointed in me. But I don't want to measure my moon with calipers, Percy. My moon was teeming with gnome folk and goddesses long before this urchin magazine was ever birthed into the world." And she holds her hand out to him. He can almost look at the magazine tenderly now, as a unit of what she is, and of the tenderness he necessarily feels for her.

This conversation needs turning around. "Do you remember," she asks, and spreads her arms with thespian overvigor, "the time in the middle of dinner when you and Lawrence started acting out the Lizzie Borden murder trial?"

"Yes! Yes! AND THREE GUESTS LEFT THE ROOM! Remember? Lawrence proved the axe committed the murder all alone, then went and buried itself in the garden. And YOU said—"

"Yes, I said 'Lawrence, stop, the guests are becoming exAXE-perated!'" Giggling. Back there in time. "And I remember the fables your Japanese friend, Tsunejiro, used to tell me. Once..."

They'll do this till the sun comes up. Let's leave the room. Let's linger while one tentative knock at the door interrupts their memoryfest, and then let's leave, let's have them continue this energizing bout of mutual solace in the dignity of private salvation.

"Yes? Lampland?"

"Yes sir."

"Come in. Well! And how did The Master Unit function?"

"Flawlessly, sir—once Tolliver repositioned your pair of chopsticks in the core, and we had the loan of Miss Lowell's tortoiseshell cigar case for a shim."

"Good. Thank you. Tell your guests to sleep well tonight. Tell them it's the closest they'll come to sleeping on Mars herself."

⌣

The Martian day is 24 hours 37 minutes 22 seconds.

The Martian day, or *padan,* is ten *zodes* (67 *padans* making a month, or *teean;* 10 *teeans,* an *ord*).

The Polar caps of Mars were first discovered by Giovanni Cassini (who later became a French subject and changed his name to Jean Dominique Cassini).

The north polar region is home to both the yellow-skinned people of Okar and the red-skinned people of Pankar; in the south polar region, the black-skinned First Born live in the Valley Dor, and the white-skinned Priests of Issus dwell in the fierce Otz Mountains.

The Viking 1 and 2 explorations of Mars have failed to prove the existence of any life on Mars, not even down to the microbial level.

Mars is Nergal, abode of Nergal, Babylonian god of death and pestilence. Mars is Pahlavani Sipher. Mars is Harmakhis. Mars is Tui (the source of the English "Tuesday"; remember the Rolling Stones song "Ruby Tuesday"?).

Mars is master of the daylight hours of Tuesday. Its metal is iron, its gem is hematite. It rules the liver, the kidney, and the left ear.

Mars invaded Earth on the night before Halloween in 1938, as reported over the radio on Mercury Theater (thousands, maybe tens of thousands, of people panic, fleeing on the highways, besieging their local police and churches, falling in fields sobbing).

Mars is just a touch over the size of the Earth (its diameter is approximately 4,200 miles) and Mars is Kepler's key to unlocking the system of planetary orbits and Mars is awash in the blood of the warring green tribes and Mars is close and then Mars is farther away then Mars is close again, with its umlaut of moons, with its emptiness and bounty.

Oh but Mars is capacious, it will hold all this and, verily, more. Like Earth, it will bear its superfluity selves with the unknowing ease of a pinhead bearing those angels—powers, thrones, and dominions of angels—that the scriptures tally in mystic numbers beyond the counting of humankind.

～

I don't know what he's like at home, with Mabel. I can only report to you that here, in his baronial guest bed, George Herriman still wears his veteran Stetson. Maybe he thinks he needs the hat to draw. He's drawing, in any case. He's leaned back on his pillow, his legs are up to act as a drawing board, he's humming a sloshy version of "Kissy Kissy Girl" around his thumb-width cigarette.

First, he sketches a few attempts at The Master Unit. Above them goes a dark bowl studded with clustered stars like generals' medals and gumball planets and cymbal moons. In a while, the Kat appears—she's never off his mind, these days—and gambols under this band of astronomical grandiosity. The Mouse appears, a wicked, sulphurous fuming in his breast; he hurls the brick...it boinks the Kat's skull...so she "sees stars," and they flitter away to join their celestial brethren and sistren…

Now it's a starry canopy, over a wedding. Herriman gives a growly laugh. You see, *he* knows—though Lou-boy doesn't yet, no Lou-boy is lost in a jambalaya of love and fear and indecision and devilish imps in his scrotum—*Herriman* knows, he can see it as plain as his own stained fingers, there's a wedding in the future, he can read the set of Rosie's jaw. She's going to clamp on that boy like a beartrap. She's going to butter him front and back and add a sprig of parsley.

And, before he *does* let sleep spill its ink through his brain, he tries a portrait of Percival Lowell, an homage to Lowell, there's no line of demarcation where the eye stops and the telescope begins. Perhaps they had an itch in common, and Herriman sensed this; his biographers say "Obsession is a major theme of Herriman's work."

And just before he sets down the pencil, he places Officer Pupp in the scene. Now Lowell spots the star on that uniformed chest, and the telescope follows it…

~

Who *is* this man—this serious, sane, astringently intelligent man—who will spend the final twenty-two years of his life insisting he's witnessed a planned-out seine of lines where NASA Mars-probe scientists say they have the on-site photographic proof that none exists?

The question deliquesces away at the edges of thought, leaving only a residue that frustrates us. We may as well ask: Who *are* these NASA scientists to say they have the proof no lines exist, where this serious, sane, intelligent man has seen them repeatedly, reading the open russet palm of Mars with probity for the final twenty-two years of his life?

"The point at issue is not whether the things reported were

actually happening, but whether they were believed to be happening, and on this point there is not a scintilla of doubt."

That's Edward Harrison, in his fine book *Masks of the Universe*. He says, "The theme of this book is that the universe in which we live, or think we live, is mostly a world of our own making. The underlying idea rests on the distinction between *Universe* and *universes*.

"The Universe is everything. What it is in it own right, independent of our changing opinions, we never know.

"The universes are our models of the Universe. They are great schemes of intricate thought—grand cosmic pictures—that rationalize human experience. *A universe is a mask fitted on the face of the unknown Universe.* Each universe determines what is perceived and what constitutes valid knowledge."

I'd like to think an accurate emblem of this world would be his telescope, an unbent reed angled up at the sky, as the turbulent murmuring currents and mists of the Hopi/Navajo spirit worlds swirl forcefully about it.

Or couldn't it simply be any two people alone together? "Alone" "together." On the oak bench at the milking shed.

"Louie, you made me the promise. You write some letters, very good; but you made me the promise. *Love, Louie* the letters say.

"*Nu?*"

∼

"The night," says Mrs. Kwakk Wakk, she of duckly mien, "it teems with moon—and promise." (George Herriman, *Krazy Kat*).

The sky is one of Arizona's most opulent effects in a while: velvety indigo, lit with long ribbons of milky incandescence. And speaking of milk: on the other side of the wall, the soft damp huffing of Venus, in some troubled sleep, keeps time. The

bell that Satellite wears around her scrawny neck is a fitful coun-
terpoint.

Louie clears his throat. Excited. Uncomfortable.

I'd like to think Rosie is somewhat stern. She's risked humiliation in coming to see him so susceptibly, she's risked the
thousand-and-one gentile confusions and degradations in wait
around every corner outside of the Lower East Side; she's worn
her three good scarves, at once, in staggered layers; she's shared
her bread with *meshúgganeh* strangers. All in all, she's earned
his deference now.

I'd like to think he offers it. I'd like to believe his time spent on
whatever psychic mission the desert represents, was healing time:
that the wine and the car and the planet maps and the cacti mean
he can step back into his own self now, on Forman Street, with
dignity, and direction.

"The cow... she was for me to milk, like in Poland."

"Now is not Poland, Louie, now is not Fleksteff, now is New
York I think, yah?"

"Yah, Rosie... you smell maybe chicken feathers?"

I'd like to think they kiss. I'd like, what the hell, to think they
kiss and the whole grand ganglionic burning show-of-shows up
there turns fireworks over their kiss, and I'd like to believe their
kiss is a contract. Yes, and before we turn our faces circumspectly
from this tryst, I'd like to think his tongue is hungrily tracing the
questionmarks that are molded, even before birth, into the
human ear.

But what do I know? — this part of the story is buried (since it's
never come up) more surely than Assyria or Babylon. I only know
that later Smuddle will show Rosie back to the main house: this
is 1912, and certain sticky proprieties must be kept. She will sleep,
she will wake, there will be a moment of wedding canopy and
then many years of depleting labor, these years will pass, she will

love, she will ache, she will croon, she will carry my mother.

⌒

Percival Lowell will live for four years more. Every night he will break himself like a wave on the sands of that red red planet. Every day he will buzz the buzz of the gadfly in the waking world's complacency.

In November 1916 he will die at the observatory. His body will be buried on Mars Hill in a mausoleum that looks like a small observatory, with a dome of transparent blue glass. His spirit— call it what you want—will ascend, along a line of obsession, to the planet Mars. The natives there will dredge him from one of the Low Canals, and expirate its waters from his lungs. He will marvel: the intricate system of locks (for some are navigable), and the lightsome boating parties!

When Amy learns of his stroke and death, the funeral will be over by a week. She's suffered a month of neuralgia, gastritis, and jaundice—with double the normal dose of morphine fuddling the pain in her body—and the house will keep this news from her until her partial recovery. So much is still ahead! The Imagism wars, and the Spectra hoax, and the ouija seance, and her book of Chinese translations, the dinners, the rollercoaster reviews of her work, the bold forays and anonymous snipings, every final ovation and snigger, all three operations on her sturdy, hurting, oil-drum of a body, every last wrung-out line of a poem… On May 12, 1925 she will look into the mirror and see the right side of her face drop. To Ada she'll simply say, "A stroke." They will gather wagons of lilacs from Sevenels's garden, surround her corpse with these, and then—at her request—she will be cremated, and the ashes consigned to the family plot at Mount Auburn. Her spirit will tunnel loose, her real self, a wee transparent flimmer. She's free, at last! And she will hover, a hummingbird, over that posthumous Pulitzer Prize, and like a hummingbird she will dart about it, supping from its sweetness. Singing the poet's song: *too late, too late.*

John Keats will consign his memory to the erasure of running water. Edgar Rice Burroughs will publish twenty-eight Tarzan novels and fourty-four other books. At Pasadena-time 4:53 A.M., July 20th, 1976, a thirteen-hundred-pound vehicle just about the size of a jeep will land on Mars on the western slopes of Chryse Planitia, 22.3 degrees north latitude and 47.5 west longitude. The sky will be salmon-pink; the soil, uniformly red. The summary Norman H. Horowitz (emeritus professor of biology at the California Institute of Technology) will provide, begins, "Viking found no life on Mars."

Louie and Rosie will live in Chicago. (The New York business will finally fail, after some exhilarating false starts; and distant relatives invite them to that booming lakeshore city.) They will raise (in order) Sally, Regina, Fannie. They will yell out their wares. She will chip Lake Michigan whitefish out of blocks of ice; and he will don his burgundy-and-epauletted organ-grinder-monkey's outfit, lifting the shoppers to toys and fixtures and ladies lingerie. At night the el will rattle their bones like dice in a godly game of chance. They will dance at the *balln*. They will do the two-backed hoochiekoo in bed. She will save the crusts of the bread, he will pick in the alley for rusted scrap and string. The girls will blossom, in their stringbean way (Regina, lost to brain cancer, eating, eating at her, like silverfish in her skull). More weddings. Grandchildren. Time will never press the *stop* switch on its turbines. He will grow hair in his ears ("gray moss!" I yelled, it became a family "cute" joke). She will pluck the bowel from the rend in the chicken one morning and see her hand is shaking. They will sit together on the porch and watch the moon, that great bronze seal of approval on the night. She will teach me to sing "In Jersey City vhere I did dvell," she will buy me a bottle of orange pop and hug me into the florid peeked-at creases of her décolletage—it's heavily shpritzed with dimestore perfume. She will enter her room in the hospital with a cheery wave and leave it without her uterus. She will wail at this all night until the sky tears down the middle like black silk, "Aiy, I'm not no voman no more." He will shrivel. She will die. He will live for a visit a week in the place they call The Home...

But all that's the future. Life is never the past, the present, or the future. Life is moments the size of the Thailand bumblebee bat that weighs less than a penny.

They're at the station now, a week later. Hearst's reporters have gone six days before (with Serviss showily unconvinced of *canali,* but bearing a furtive respect for his host's well-marshaled zeal). Herriman said, "Lou-boy, you're a genuine ring-tailed prodigy," and hugged him and ostentatiously smooched on Rosie. "Here," he gave Louie a piece of paper, folded and taped, "to open later. And here," a separate piece, "my newspaper telephone number. I know a place that seasons its egg foo yung with lightning." But of course they never did get together, back in New York.

Then Louie had spent six days at his round of menial tasks while Smuddle searched out a replacement. Lowell took Amy and Rosie picnicking into the desert. Rosie attempted a cigarillo. Amy learned the words to *Bah mir bist du shayn.* Louie had given Lowell a present, a child's toy he'd purchased at Larcher's, that Lowell removed from his briefcase now: a pair of rose-tinted spectacles. Looking around: the sands were red. This is what it would be like.

When the train pulled into the station, there was an all-around formal shaking of hands. Then Louie pinched Rosie's bottom, for show. "Jews," thought Lowell. "You have the monies?" asked

Amy. Rosie nodded. (For the recipe, from Mrs. Larcher's private coffers, and gratefully paid out.) "Mine friends," said Louie, clearing his throat and feeling important, "about the good-bye. Ve haff a saying from mine people—" but the train whistle lowed, and they ran off in a rhythm of his duffle bag and her hat box.

That night, while Rosie dozed, he untaped George's drawing. He was standing under a canopy, holding Rosie's hand, and the sky was crammed with six-pointed Jewish stars.

In the corner, that Coconino feline gave a frolicsome leap and clicked her heels. "Be heppa," she said.

～

He will kronikle the kanon of the Kat every day until April 25, 1944. Dropsy, migraine, arthritis. "I remember my aunt putting glass tubes in his legs, to draw off the water." He once said that he wanted to end his life in Monument Valley in Arizona "lying down on a cactus leaf until I was shrivelled up and blown away by the wind." In respect of his wishes, his ashes were scattered over the Navajo reservation of Monument Valley.

> *Homeward now shall I journey,*
> *Homeward upon the rainbow;*
> *In Life Unending, and beyond it,*
> *Yea, seated at home behold me.*

～

"Ve go home now," Louie gratuitously said, by way of indicating his deeply whole-hearted endorsement of their confluent travel back to New York. They watched the miles re-ravel back up.

He felt like a monarch. He'd had an adventure! He'd won his woman! And, *ssh*, he had an idea too, a winner of an idea.

Lenses.

Louie had seen the future.

When they were back, he thought, he'd have a few ambitious suggestions to share with Nate.

~

Science-fantasy emir Ray Bradbury writes of his coming under the spell of Edgar Rice Burroughs when he was ten: "For how can one resist walking out of a summer night to stand in the middle of one's lawn to look up at the red fire of Mars quivering in the sky and whisper: *Take me home.*"

The Future

*W*hen I was five or six—so this would be around 1954—we'd drive out to the airport on occasional weekend nights, for entertainment. It was cheap, that may have been its primary lure—my parents were ever-scrabbling lower-middle-class citizens; an entire evening of family fun for the price of airport parking couldn't be naysaid. And it wasn't, after all, *any* airport; no, this was O'Hare, the parvenu of airports, and the great gray slab that welcomed you as you came in off the expressway proclaimed its globally special status: "The World's Busiest Airport." Forked around my father's neck, onto his shoulders, straining to see the far red winks of celestial tonnage.

But it wasn't just their fearful monthly battle with expenses— my parents weren't *settling for* second-best, in an effort to scrimp. The complicated pageantry of O'Hare was truly wondrous to them, and its foreign ports of call (Los Angeles, Pittsburgh...), truly exotic. There were men in immaculate uniforms, who knew the secrets by which these flying battleships touched down like windowledge pigeons. There were women out of the movies—high heels and troweled-on eyelinered sidelong looks—whose lives were as large as flight plans. You could see a man in a turban! Mysterious lights blinked, people were paged from out of nowhere into private glamour or tragedy, and of course there were the planes themselves, humming on the runways with self-confidence and brio.

It would be twenty more years before my parents flew on one, and this they'd relate with a child's pleasure, overplaying their vaunted calm at takeoff, repeating endlessly the distinction of being served kosher meals, saving the in-flight magazine as if they were hauling back moon rocks. My mother seemed a bit more unflappable; but I believe if they'd offered my father the chance to wear a *Junior Pilot* badge and enter the cockpit, he'd have reached out for the stewardess's slender hand as innocently as a child and happily entered that compact wonderland of dials and gauges.

So you can see how splendor-struck they must have been on those weekend outings, even knowing perfectly well (they weren't *terminally* naive) that life had declared them the two-bit extras, the background players, in other people's intercontinental dramas. Surrounded by five-star potentates and paramours blasé with travel, my parents—only minimally matriculated from *their* parents' world—would walk around as if Kitty Hawk had been that very morning, and now they were magically being permitted a glimpse of the future.

Yes, *that's* what I'm trying to say. For them, this was the future (thinly disguised as workaday hustle-bustle)—as *I* was the future for them, I suppose, the better tomorrow they counted on, the promise and the hope (although disguised as a tired, petulant five-year-old boy-child, asking can we go home now).

⁓

In the spring of 1912 Picasso did three paintings incorporating the cover of a tri-color brochure "exhorting France to improve its military aviation," *Notre Avenir est dans l'air,* "Our Future is in the Air." According to Varnedoe and Gopnick, Picasso and Braque "were both caught up in the general public infatuation with aviation." Beyond that, they were first exploring painting-*cum*-collage, and using ephemera—bits of newspaper headline, foil, string—on their canvases; and so, with Kitty Hawk in mind, they "may have felt a special affinity with the way the collaborating Wrights had made a decisive leap of invention with extremely simple means, rethinking basic principles and using parts available to anyone."

Biplanes! Triplanes! Propellers! A word like *aeronautical!* It all seems excitingly forward-looking. But really this was the past already.

In 1912 the cover of Hugo Gernsback's magazine *Modern Electrics* showed the hero "Ralph 124C 41+" seated at the wheel of his spaceship, pioneering the stars (the wheel is intriguingly transparent, and his viewport is surrounded by gizmoesque gadgetry). *Science Fiction* is Gernsback's coinage. But Verne had sent his voyagers on *A Trip from the Earth to the Moon* as early as 1866, and while his cannon-shot projectile might not qualify as a spaceship in the strictest sense, by 1880 Percy Greg is following *his* adventurers *Across the Zodiac* —powered in a true ship by the mysterious force he calls "apergy." In 1900 George Griffith writes *A Honeymoon in Space.* Its illustration shows the wedded twosome mawkishly holding hands and staring out of their spaceship window at astral dazzlement. (Meanwhile they're dressed in the very honeymoon best of Victorian finery.)

The future has been here a long, long time.

I stop for a drink at the local strip joint. Usually it's simple peel-and-pose, but sometimes there's the more elaborate semblance of a skit. Tonight, the ladies perform a campy *"Flesh" Gordon,* relishing their lively eroticization of the original's plodding derring-do. Although the costumes are minimal, there's enough for them to signify "the world of tomorrow": silverplated shoulderwings; deco, antennaed helmets; zap guns shooting forth horrible hypno-rays.

It's *intended* to say "tomorrow." What it really *does* say is "nostalgia." The first *Flash Gordon* Sunday comic strip appeared on January 7, 1934.

~

Exactly five years before, to the day, on January 7, 1929, *Buck Rogers* premiered—the prototype s.f. strip. Now when I say *Flash Gordon* was the past, I *mean* the past: Flash blasted off from Earth in 1934 in a bulky 1934 spaceship, and whatever compelling faux-futuristic look the hardware and partywear of his adventures had was simply due to prevailing styles on Mongo, the planet to which he, Dale Arden, and Dr. Zarkov voomed their way.

But Buck was accidentally deep-freezed over time (I should be accurate: the gas of a sudden mine accident preserved him), and his exploits took place (*will* take place?) (you see the loopy confusions…) in the twenty-fifth century. *This* was the stuff! The Strato-Smasher, the Parallo-Scope, the Electro-Beam, the Invisibility Turbine, the Transimmobilizer.

That was the bristling armorial claptrap clattering in my head the day I rescued Dottie Yenkel from certain doom.

I was ten, and solitary; the Sunday comics must have been a primary source of companionship, at the least a permanent backdrop to my own days out in the world.

And she was—eight, nine? (I remember even later, when I was seventeen or so, she still seemed eight or nine, a girl who flirted with mild childlike retardation the way the other neighborhood girls were already reeling in womanhood from the future, holding it close to them like a voodoo doll, then swaying out to torture the neighborhood boys with their new-learnt musky fashionability. And there Dottie would be, on her porch, in a frump dress—playing, still, with the yarn loops of her potholder maker, singing to herself. It was easy to picture her on the porch this way for sixty more years.)

The day was clear and quiet. This was down by the trashdump piles, along that doodle of water we called "the lagoon." I heard some shouts—not hers, though: she was only snuffling—then I crested a lump of stunted grass and saw her, on the dirt, surrounded by three boys slightly older than I was, thirteen, fourteen, old enough to have that juiced-up hankering in them. You know what I mean.

You know it better than I knew then, I didn't know much of the world then, what I did know would have fit giftwrapped in a single Sunday comics page. I suppose that's an accurate symbol of my psyche at work, and I was Buck Rogers, she was the lithesome and clearly imperiled Wilma Deering, words like *valiant* and *gallant* must have been twitting around inside my skull, the size of mosquitoes but spitting fire like rocket jets. I ran down the slope with a pitiful war cry, fists in a windmill, straight at the leering, slavering Evil Spawn.

When I came to—I'm sure it wasn't more than a minute—they were gone. Perhaps they really *had* run off in fear—the fear they'd killed me. I wished they had. There wasn't a cuticle, a hair, that didn't ache. My nose was bleeding, it felt like little more than a tablespoon of mush dropped onto my face. But there was Dottie at least, still hunkered on the dirt as I'd last seen her, only safe now, safe because of me. Laboriously, as if assembling a model kit, I rose myself to my feet, then held my hand out to her, my rescued damsel.

She screamed. It split that air like a ripped linen. Then—these happened simultaneously—she turned in a panic and ran, she was gone in an instant; and I realized, as if my defeat hadn't cost me enough, that her shriek had not only left my poor heart palpitating crazily on the back of my tongue, but loosed my bladder.

And so I stood there a while, feeling my pee begin to cool around my crotch and down my legs. Another adventure of Space Commander Goldbarth in The Land of the Future.

~

The grasses the hunt the dark and then the grasses the hunt the dark and then…

If "future" means foreseeing change, there must have been a time—the species' major time—when there wouldn't have been a future; when time was replica, not revolution; when anything that *could* ever happen, *had* happened; and when birth then aging then death took place inside the greater present tense.

Or as Thomas Mann says, of the days of Babylonia, of Ur: "Six hundred years at that time and under that sky did not mean what they mean in our western history. They were a more level, silent, speechless reach; time was less effective, a more unified and thus briefer vista."

Though once the future exists at all, no matter how distant and nebular, it doesn't lie in wait—it flings itself headlong against the grain of time to meet us. My grandmother standing at Ellis Island, fresh off the boat, the scummy verminous belowdecks of which she'd entered fresh off the horsecart—standing there, holding her frayed cloth bag: 1903: at Kitty Hawk, North Carolina, Orville and Wilbur Wright are flying. She'd live to see

Sputnik. Gutting the just-plucked carcass for a chicken soup so bobbled by gnarled eldritch contents it could be Atlantean in recipe, she'd live to see Sputnik and only four years later my bar mitzvah, which was future aplenty for her, and so she died.

But *I* wasn't going to die. No, I was thirteen and I was going to live forever! I was thirteen, I was fried each day in the alternating current of cocksure swagger and inadequacy. I dreamed. I stormed. I played with my dick, my impetuous other. I wondered: God, sure, okay, why not, but who made *God* then? I practiced a sullen stare. My brain wasn't big enough for my body, my body wasn't big enough for my ravenous heart, my heart would have *drooled* if I'd held it up to the light. It would bounce. Hell, *I* could bounce, like a man on the moon one-sixth the weight blah blah. I'd get a tattoo. I'd weep for the starving. I'd win the admiration of Phyllis Kirschenbaum, third row, fourth seat, our tongues would squirm the squirm of mating snails.

At night I gawked at the covers of pulp mags—*Startling Wonder Stories, Amazing, Superscience Monthly*—staring as if my eyes could knock against that tacky artwork like two knuckles, and I'd be admitted. There were pitted, fire-coned planet landscapes, soared across by the regalmost armadas of patrolling rockets, and populated chiefly by women so perfect their bodies were pure Euclidean shapes befleshed, and then the flesh beglittered in the crisscrossed silver spaghetti-straps of "thermo-cling," which seemed to be the loose, louche fashion choice of space seductresses. I wasn't stupid and *still* I'd tilt those covers as if a different angle might let me ogle a bosom better.

I wouldn't have known that famous statement of Lincoln Steffens's (made for such a different purpose) but I'd have signed on board its ringing sentiment for a lifelong term: "I have seen the future, and it works."

We all want our share. That night in the strip joint, a couple of sharply-creased young stockbrokers try to score with two of the dancers, explaining that they speculate, they *buy up* futures; twenties get rubbed between their fingers like lotion. And the dancers are going *ooh* and eyeing the greenery: they also have to think about tomorrow.

On my weavy way out I pass two nerd computer types who aren't even watching the floor show, no, they're talking excitedly to one another, byte-log and recall and cross-screen memory transfer, things that I won't *vaguely* know about for years. They're on the crest of the wave, and they know it. They're hip to the *next* wave. They're in on the coming thing.

∽

It doesn't seem so rosy, though, to watch a knot of garbage pickers squabble over a cat's head—for the winner, it will be his only meat all week, and maybe he'll hustle it home to leach the supercilious essence of cat brain into a stew for days on end, or maybe he'll only zigzag to a shitted-up cellar he knows of, where he'll crack that skull against a ledge and feast on the whole of it right there with his fingers.

This is the future too, or a possible future, credibly scried in scenes from an actual now. The current *Newsweek* coolly piles global warming gloom on gloom, and adds to that the rest of the countdown facts we've learned to love to fear: the lethal doilying of the ozone layer; seemingly unstoppable Malthusian math; the weekly winking out of up to 500 species; the crying of forests; the gasping throes of the ocean itself. In 1991 over *three million* children were dead of diarrheal disease—let's strap each one to the shoulders of somebody somewhere ordering a Perrier-and-lime. Let's strap it on until the face bursts like the back of a ruptured sofa: *that's* the future. That's the egg-laying bug that's eaten its way through the eardrum. Atmospheric carbon dioxide will double over the next 100 years. World population will more than double. Entire tribal units shaving the cheek-meat off trapped feral cats.

It's *Newsweek* but it isn't news—this future has been with us from Bosch and Breugel through *Mad Max,* grubbily medieval and forever setting up shop just blocks away from where the streets are paved with gold. We like to fancy that "the future" means ongoingness, but in the dumps of Catville it may simply be that waking up means smacking into a brick wall every day.

And it must be, too, that we've all felt the personal version of this: the hopelessness of knowing where it all ends up, no matter the monastic candelabrum-flames of the soul or the funkier sudsing delights of the glands. So that, when they lowered my father into the broken winter earth, I understood at last (as if I'd been a slow student, but this was my breakthrough) the answer is always zero when we've added up a life.

He'd taught me, time and again, the line that separates welcome moxie from insolence; he'd taught me the common homily of his generation of men, that The Addition of an Undershirt Believe It Or Not Keeps You Cooler, "by absorbing the sweat"; he'd comforted me, in my rube humiliation at the Annual Company Picnic games… And now what?—here he was, his own best sales pitch for Metropolitan Life Insurance's fistful-of-pennies immigrant plan, that he peddled (and purchased himself) for three—no, more than three—decades of worn shoe leather. Here he was, the future he'd duly predicted in third-floor walk-up living rooms all those laboring years.

That night, the softness of a mother overcomes hardheaded truth; my sister predicates for Lindsay Nichol, my niece, age three, an afterlife of vaguely-conjured familial reunion. "He's with *his* mommy now" is what I remember. It takes its flimmery, momentary place in The Great Attempt. "As far back as the ancient world," say McDannell and Lang (and so far as I can tell from recent magazine polls, straight up to the cockamamie moment) "belief in life after death was widespread, considered normal, and not generally weakened by skepticism."

So: does Lindsay believe it? Do her frightened, truly *gushed,* tears mean she believes it? Whether yes or no, it seems we're neurally wired for such belief. Jacob Bronowski: "There comes a stage in a child's life, before he is twelve months old, when he visibly takes the great step. Before this stage, if you show a child a toy and then put it behind your back, his interest disappears: he is not aware of objects that are not in his actual field of sensation. And then one day there comes a moment when the child is aware that the toy behind your back is still a toy—it is still somewhere, it exists, and it will return."

And so, the threshold we find at Neanderthal sites: for the first time, burial rites imply transcendence. The teenage corpse at Le Moustier is arranged as if sleeping, and set in a scatter of bones of wild cow. The woman at La Ferrassie is exaggeratedly folded into the fetal position. Especially I like the young child of Teshik Tash, who's heading into the Earth, and maybe beyond the Earth, through a careful ring of six pairs of ibex bones.

~

"The toy behind your back... is still somewhere, it exists, and it will return." My living room is aheap with *return:* hundreds of representatives of the merry Mouse and dyspeptic Duck of Disneyana, gleaming in glazed ceramic or lithographed tin; the plastic icons of various advertising animal gods from my childhood, Froggy Gremlin (shoes) and the Red Goose (also shoes), the Bosco Bear (a chocolate syrup), Elsie the Cow (whose happily proffered squirts of milk became, presumably, the matrix in which the Bosco was stirred); a toy typewriter; rust-specked

wind-up trains or buses (some no more than the width of a nickel) tracking their way through miniature oblong landscapes of
Scheherazadean intricacy and color…

If we dote on things, are we in our dotage? If so, then I'm
admittedly the dotard of these objects I've collected from out of
the midden dump of Time, and set in a splendid arrested childhood on my shelves.

One corner is busy enacting the future. Spaceships, saucerfied
to be as round as birthday cakes, or done up in the bulbous style
of aerodynamically-masted bratwursts. Ray guns (or zap guns
or sonic blaster guns or atomic flash guns: they were cranked out
in hundreds of models), often decorated goofily in "space motif,"
in planets ringed by sturdy golden hoops, in shooting stars that
trail blazing streamers of speed behind them. Bubble-helmeted,
rocket-jalopying paladins of the spacelanes. We would conquer
the distantmost reaches of the unknown, we would seed ourselves in its glories. We would keep the peace of alien stellar na-
tions, we would zip like metal midges through that air. My Rex
Mars Playset is an entire port of call, with upthrust starliners,
astral viewing domes, and pylons ready to crackle out the snaky
jolts of weird fission it takes to reach the rim of the universe.

The amazing thing is, I live in that future. I'm half-way into
1992, and by the best forecasting standards of 1956, I should be
using my I.D.-tronics code to have my robo-butler telebeam
reservations for my wife and myself on the lunar cruiser to
Moondome City this weekend, but I assure you (as I sit here
waiting word from the garage, on my doddering six-cylinder
Dodge) I am not.

I check the covers again, of *Galaxy, Astounding, Worlds of If*—
they never prophesied AIDS, or cities buzzed asunder by crack
and meth; they couldn't imagine talk shows favoring tales of
sexual abuse or waste recycling, over the triumph of claiming

Orion and the Pleiades. It was 1956 and we could send a crew of Space Cadets to mingle with fellow Cadets from planets of four-armed beings and tentacled beings and sea-bred beings whose helmets were goldfish-bowl-like filled with nutritive water—and never once picture a Negro Cadet in the midst of our own Caucasian fold.

I can't even see it as wrong, so much as horribly innocent. *That,* I think, is the corner's appeal: those snappy designs, and their failure, held in balance. We'd shoot a rocket crew at f.t.l. (that's "faster than light"), exploring the shores of worlds half-a-cosmos away, and when they landed they'd reach in their spacesuit pockets, to write down the aliens' first words with a stubby pencil and paper pad.

Such are the limits of vision. Or maybe it's fairer to simply say this is a viable *new* vision, a recognition of present and future as inseparable mix. In 1956 the Institute for Contemporary Art, in London, opened its exhibit "This *Is* Tomorrow" (my emphasis); greeting the gallery-goers was a larger-than-life-size reproduction of Robby the Robot bearing a fainted blonde starlet in his arms (this, lifted from "Hollywood's most Freudian vision of outer space," *Forbidden Planet).* Just in front, like an ocean wave into which Robby was stolidly wading, were the gust-blown skirts of Marilyn Monroe in *The Seven-Year Itch.* These images introduced a curving panorama of scenes from movies in Cine-maScope—as if the latest word in entertainment, and our inter-galactic travel, were parts of the same unparsable, glittering block of ability and aesthetic. (On my Rex Mars shelf, those rockets *are* the tailfinned Buicks of 1956, set tilted starward.)

Isn't *that* what I was to my parents, slipping my sleeping body out of the Buick's patched back seat (we're home now from the airport), bringing me gently to bed?—the future, yes, but ("Albie, we'll get your teacher a little Christmas gift: you have to learn the ways of the world if you want to get along") the future cast in the only terms they knew (or anyone ever knows), the unavoidable terms of the now-gestalt. No matter what the maestroseers—Ezekiel, Cassandra, Nostradamus—might claim, the gypsy's crystal is surely no more than a lens that's folded over itself repeatedly, so immediacy is intensified into its own best possible guess.

The Dodge is out of the shop. It's 2 A.M., I'm driving the streets of Wichita, Kansas, thinking these things. I'm seeing a boy, embarrassed—as he knew he'd be, as he loudly predicted he'd be—in front of the class with a fake gold ashtray in his hands (you rested the cigarette in the open beak of a fake gold crow) inscribed FOR MR. WALLY (who was thankful though, it turned out, didn't smoke). I'm thinking, I'm driving, I'm smiling, I'm choking emotionally, I'm shaking my head.

I drive up through the Boeing plant. At 2 A.M. it's lit up as bright as by day. At a distant hangar, tiny men are crawling about inside the on-view cockpit framework of some huge commercial airliner, looking like struggling thoughts in a dinosaur's brain.

Will we travel the stars? Perhaps. But it will take science enough to merely clean the skies of my Dodge's emissions.

What does the present *ever* know? Near dawn, it turns foggy. I drive myself into a mound of fog like a word headed into erasure.

∼

One night I attended a fund-raising dinner. Not black-tie-required, but chichi nevertheless. A woman whose work I respected was giving the keynote address. An entire stylishly-tailored service network of women in her profession surrounded her, grooming her, fueling her, fending off trouble. Later there were drinks and everyone loosened up a little. Hello, I'd like you to meet, how pleased I am, excuse me do you know, names scampered past. One lady there—a Dorothy Chavez, I was told—I saw did a breath-taking job of retaining the icy composure of the bright white-collar professional, yet still ferociously flirted with the power men in the room. I could see that she liked this—someone for whom the word "control" becomes a totem idea.

Eventually we were introduced. "You know," she said, "I *wanted* to be there, that day. I was exploring my sexuality." I stared at her like a dope. "I was showing them..." studied silence "...things." And then the glimmer broke through me. Dorothy, Dottie. ("Dottie, meet Dopey....") Dottie Yenkel, from when I was ten.

She'd taken her husband's name in the last of the days when a woman *could,* and not feel simpering; and she'd kept it, now that it was so politically advantageous a moniker, after the divorce.

So much for my career as a prophet. Albert Goldbarth, Reader of Souls.

So much for my scruples and clear-headed will. We went to bed that night—she'd taken a room in the same ritz-dripping hotel that had sponsored the dinner. I can't guess why she seized *me,* from that range of mighty talkers—what reliving or renouncing of her past our single night was meant to accomplish. And I can't guess why I acquiesced, although her silk-sheathed body suggested a carnal Louvre of charms, and her wit performed on occasion the nimble leaps of elegant thimble-hoofed mountain goats; and in those days, let's face it, I didn't say no to tenderness, especially sexual tenderness, or even to its momentary feignment, it was in such short supply.

But *why* isn't the point; there's no point, really, there's only two of us, emptied on the sweated-up sheets of four in the morning, with sex's cooling stickiness and the dark dregs of the night in us the way two glasses hold the coating residue of their bourbon. She's on her stomach, and muttering; almost asleep, and muttering—successes she's had, successes she'd been cheated out of, scraplets of intended humor, whatever. I'm weary and stroking her back. The simplest thoughts seem wrapped in a soiled gauze.

And I keep marveling at it: how far I've come to be here; Dottie too. How far, how faster than light, to be at the side of this alien creature, taking in her words with my pencil's-worth of comprehension.

~

For Madame Sophyra, the future would seem to be a chart of the human palm, dotted-lined and labeled like the steer in a butcher shop poster.

For the socialite and her tiresome beau, it's a marble staircase, bannistered in brass with gilded fleurs-de-lys, and ever easing upward.

It might be the collapse, itinerary-taking, and then reflowering of the entire cosmos itself. It might be the casting (hence "forecasting"?) of ritual pig knuckles scribbled with deific imprecations. Or it might be the Voice that spoke to Noah: a microchip of God in the brain.

But for most of us, it's more like another spirit-withering day on the assembly line, producing, by our partite contributions, next year's model.

This prognostication, Bronowski says, is one of the inarguable signs of (and original neural steps toward) our humanity.

"The earliest instance of foresight that we know," he says, "is probably the presence of pebbles and worked stones in the limestone caves of australopithecus. The pebbles are not improvisations…(but) were picked up by the australopithecus in the river gravel and carried some miles to his cave, and that implies a clear intention to use them as tools. This display of foresight has rightly been taken by Oakley, Washburn, and others as a crucial step in the evolution of intelligence."

Where does it begin? Well, "somewhere near the level of the primates, a number of the direct response paths of lower animals were lengthened by being switched through the new brain: the effect was to delay the response." This delay, essentially this ability to mull over a thought, became what Bronowski terms *internalization*. "When language is internalized, it ceases to be only a means of social communication, and is thereby removed from the family of animal languages. It now becomes an instrument of reflection and exploration. In time, sentences lose the character of (mere) messages, and become experimental arrangements of the images of past experience into new and untested projections."

And so the worked pebble exists in Time: it becomes "not only a tool but a blueprint."

Here they are, for their first bow, stepping out of the prehistoric shadows and into the full light of history: human beings. "They can recall the past and manipulate the imagery of recall to construct hypothetical situations. They have a sense of the future."

Here we are, in our hungry and knowingly mortal human skins, considering next week's pork belly market, second-guessing the TV weather lady yammering there in her sexy galoshes and slicker, saving despairingly toward retirement, waiting the lab report on the marrow samples so painfully, so *casually* and painfully, forced out of the targeted bone.

My wife's friend Helen Brewer was born in 1913; Kitty Hawk was only ten years gone. This year, at age seventy-nine, she and her husband Joe drove over to Jericho Springs, Missouri, in a (finally failed) attempt to fill in genealogical blank space in the life of Joe's paternal grandfather, who'd died in a holdup in Jericho Springs, in a time and a place so poor in records-keeping it might as well be misty time B.C. we're talking about.

"We were the only people checked into the Jericho Springs Motel that night," she says, and winks with an old people's slyly self-deprecatory joke: "So we could make as much noise as we wanted."

As always, Helen and Joe turned up their share of anecdotal sprightliness, including being hosted by a local man who'd raised for a hobby 500 kinds of cactus. There was no luck in tracing the grandfather's fate, but they did track down a lady who remembered Joe's father. She was a hundred and three, and blind, and on her back in a nursing home. Once a week "her man friend," ninety-two, visited her from the farmstead that he still worked, living alone there—"and wouldn't you know it, the place was as neat as a pin!"

Listening to it—Skyler's thirty-seven now and I'm forty-four. Listening, looking fascinatedly into that chrono-mirror. That's what Buck Rogers would call it: a "Chrono-mirror." But we have a time machine, Skyler and I, that Buck and Flash can't begin to imagine.

And every morning we wake from its keeping, moved ahead inexorably by an increment of eight hours.

~

After the War, Japan became a clutterscape of discarded American tin: beer, canned goods, other tossed container trash. What they craftily did (or "cannily" did, I could say) was recycle it as cheaply-made toys for export. Forty years later, these are avidly sought by those with an eye for their zingy appeal. The intricate ones are truly inventive and jolly: Mr. Fox the magician places his top hat over an egg, removes the hat with panache, and—!!—*there's a chicken.* The bartender mixes a drink, pours, sips, smacks lips, then his nose lights up and his ears smoke.

Tin is especially right for rocketships and ray guns, since it emulates (as plastic, say, or wood, or cloth, would not) the look of the "actual" material in the "real world's" ray gun or rocketship. Tin takes the lithography brightly, too, in a special way unduplicated in other toys, and the aqua-blue we commonly associate with the 1950's (and frequently seen in diner design, in boomerang ashtrays, in "kit-kat" wall clocks, etc.) is the perfect "outer-space-blue" blue for these kinds of toys, and for the red and yellow flames and meteors and electrical bolts that would always seem to be whizzing across their surface.

"It is getting harder & harder to find this swell stuff. I have quite a pile already but I love these toys and must have MORE MORE MORE," wrote Barbara Moran to me—she's a dealer and collector—in a note that came with the "Futuristic EXPLORER Car (Has Several Spacemen Looking Out Of Windows)" I'd ordered. A swell swell thing.

We all have our tales of triumph and travail, we collectors. On a trip out to visit Jimbo in Boston, I'd chanced (in three successive stops) on three extraordinary space guns, screamingly blue and looking as if they were meant to be collected into this set of triplets all along. It really seemed enchanted, and that spell was still upon me when I gingerly packed them into my squooshable carry-on case, each one in a wadded-up pair of dirty undershorts, then each wad coddled in crumpled paper, then each of those in its plastic bag.

And it had been a good visit as well in other ways, but now I was weary, and anxious for getting back to wife and work. I know I felt bedraggled. I know my left leg ached. And none of that mattered, leaving Boston; but unconcernedly walking self and goodies through security in Kansas City was something else.

The moment those first faint scrolls of suspicion distorted the lips of the x-ray guard, it hit me. Of course: these trinkets of mine would show the silhouettes of real, working guns. "Oh those are only—" was all I said, and a bell went off, and three enormous Protectors of Civilized Life surrounded me, each with *his* hand dancing like a spider on the butt-end of *his* real and working gun, and by *this* time a crowd had gathered to witness the miscreant terrorist receive his come-uppance as one by one my balled-up dirty undershorts were brought forth for their public perusal and one by one my innocent, delicate, eminently scratchable droppable Boston baubles were held forth for their public disdain, and I was sleepless, ache-shot, rumpled, hobbling, and because it was an airport, I guess—the "airportness" is what must have done it—I saw him there, as if six feet of drear Chicago earth were only one more door on his route, and a voice from somewhere inside me, a voice deep-freezed and then thawed alive in this slippery world of tomorrow, asked "Can we go home now?"

Notes

DELFT

Browsings through a number of books have obviously helped me make these, my own small leaps. Brendan Lehane's fascinating *The Compleat Flea* (New York: Viking Press, 1969) was indispensable. From a number of sources cited in-text, I'd also like to single out Clifford Dobbell's *Antony van Leeuwenhoek and His "Little Animals"* (New York: Russell & Russell, 1958); Brian J. Ford's *Single Lens: The Story of the Simple Microscope* (New York: Harper & Row, 1985); and Leonard J. Slatkes's *Vermeer and His Contemporaries* (New York: Abbeville Press, 1981).

> *Er Klert, tsi a floy hot a pupik.*
> (He wonders if a flea has a bellybutton.)
> YIDDISH PROVERB

∼

THE HISTORY OF THE UNIVERSE IS IMPORTANT TO THIS STORY

Tycho Brahe and Johannes Kepler did know Rabbi Loew of the Golem legends. Brahe's last words are indeed supposed to be those to Kepler as here reported. But this is obviously not intended as an historical document, and it veers from "historical" "facts" as it needs. Similarly, my quotations from various texts sometimes take small liberties, for purposes of rhythm or concision; while I try to remain true to content and style, quotations may be minimally abbreviated, reworded, or patchworked together. I hope this seems more good use, and less abuse, because I am (among many incidental sources) particularly indebted to the following books: Angus Armitage, *John Kepler;* Nathan Ausubel (ed.), *A Treasury of Jewish Folklore;* John Banville, *Kepler;* Chayim Block, *The Golem: Mystical Tales from the Ghetto of Prague;* Evan S. Connell, *The White Lantern;* Mircea Eliade, *The Quest: History and Meaning in Religion;* Richard Grossinger, *The Night Sky;* Lyall Watson, *Beyond Supernature*; Colin Wilson, *Starseekers.*

From the Schocken Books edition of *Zohar: Basic Readings from the Kabbalah:*

> Once Rabbi Eleazar and Rabbi Abba were sitting
> together, and then the dusk came. Going, they
> beheld two stars speed toward each other from
> different points of the sky, meet, and then vanish.
> "Who fathoms it, how these two stars come from
> different points, how they meet and disappear?"

∼

WORLDS

Fact and fancy blend here, I hope as interestingly as do Terran and Barsoomian. Quotations from sources are sometimes slightly altered for reasons of concision or rhythm. That tampering admitted, let me go on to pay gratitude to the following books: William Graves Hoyt, *Lowell and Mars;* John Noble Wilford, *Mars Beckons;* S. Foster Damon,

Notes

Amy Lowell, A Chronicle; Jean Gould, *Amy;* C. David Heymann, *American Aristocracy;* Douglas Bush, *John Keats;* John Flint Roy, *A Guide to Barsoom;* Irwin Porges, *Edgar Rice Burroughs, the Man Who Created Tarzan;* McDonnell, O'Connell and De Havenon, *Krazy Kat, the Comic Art of George Herriman* (& quoting Gilbert Seldes); Eclipse Books, *Ignatz and Krazy* (various volumes' introductory materials); Robert M. Quinn, "Krazy's Dad: George Herriman and Krazy Kat" (in *Artspace*); Franklin Rosemont, "George Herriman (Krazy Kat)" (in *Cultural Correspondence*); Joseph Campbell, *The Inner Reaches of Outer Space* (& quoting Natalie Curtis); Kirk Varnedoe and Adam Gopnick, *High & Low: Modern Art and Popular Culture;* Edward T. Hall, *The Dance of Life;* Evan S. Connell, *The White Lantern;* Edward Harrison, *Masks of the Universe.*

∼

THE FUTURE

This essay thankfully makes use of materials from Varnedoe and Gopnik, *High & Low;* McDannell and Lang, *Heaven: A History;* and Bronowski, *A Sense of the Future.* Quoted material may bear small alterations for purposes of rhythm or concision.

ABOUT THE AUTHOR

Albert Goldbarth lives in Wichita, Kansas, where he is Distinguished Professor of Humanities at Wichita State University. His collections of poems have been appearing for over two decades and include, among others, *Jan 31* (nominated for the National Book Award), *Heaven and Earth* (recipient of the National Book Critics Circle Award) and, most recently, *Across the Layers: Poems Old and New*. His earlier selection of essays, from Coffee House Press, is *A Sympathy of Souls*.